JN033448

Noh 5 Scripts in English

― 対訳能五番 ―

中野洋介
Nakano Yosuke

文芸社

Contents

序 文

　もう7、8年も前の事です。その頃私は65歳でリタイアした後専ら海外旅行をもっと楽しもうとして始めた英語が段々面白くなり、多読英語をやったり、英会話教室に通ったり、TOEICに挑戦したりしていたのでした。

　その日大阪府藤井寺市の自宅近くの英会話教室では受講者が順に自分のライフワークか何かを発表するセッションをやっていて、私が能の話をするとカナダから来た中年の男性講師が自分も日本の古典芸能に関心があり、能に興味を持っている、と言いました。そして能は言葉は分からなくても、見聞きするだけで面白いけれど、もしも英訳のスクリプトのようなものがあると助かるのだが…と言ったのです。その言葉は素人上がりの能楽師範で、能を職業としている訳ではない私にとって、心にピンと響くものがありました。ここに私に出来る重要なことがあると思ったのです。

　それ以降、英語と能という観点で色々と文献を調べました。先ず檜書店から発行されている『A Guide to Noh』という小冊子があります。文庫本サイズの260頁ほどの小さな本ですが、能全般の解説と能200番余の簡単な解説が載っています。巻末に外国語に翻訳された能本の紹介があり、そこで私はArthur Waley（1910 ～ 1966）の『The Noh Plays of Japan』（TUTTLE PUBLISHING）を知りました。能19番を完訳しています。Arthur Waleyは「源氏物語」の英訳「The Tale of Genji」で知られる東洋学者だけあって、その英訳能は簡潔且つ詩的で、あたかも「謡」*を吟ずる如きリズム感がある一方、やや表現が抽象的すぎる印象を受けました。本格的な英訳能としてはもう一つ、日本学術振興会訳の『The Noh Drama-Ten Plays from the Japanese』

Preface

It was when I attended an English conversation school near my house in Fujiidera City, seven to eight years ago, that a middle-aged English teacher from Canada mentioned Noh scripts being written in English for foreign audiences of Japanese Noh plays. At that time, I was very interested in studying English, which I started simply for the purpose of better enjoying my travels abroad after my retirement at the age of 65. I then tried to learn extensive reading in English, kept studying at the school for English conversation, and started taking TOEIC tests.

One day, we had a class in which we had to make a presentation about our own dreams or life's work, and I told my classmates about my Noh performances. The teacher then commented, saying, "I like watching Noh plays. It's enjoyable enough just to watch the performances, but if there were English scripts, it would be much more enjoyable."

The thought struck me : I was a Noh instructor with a background as an amateur, as opposed to being a professional performer. Because of this, I was also apt to devote myself to the things other than Noh itself, like studying English, and I thought that here is a task where I can really make a contribution to the ongoing prosperity of Noh, through providing a means to disseminate Noh theater worldwide.

After that, I started to look into various existing materials related to Noh being written in English.

First, there was a booklet called "A Guide to No", published by a publisher specializing in Noh, Hinoki Shoten. It was a pocket-sized book of about 260 pages, including a general explanation of Noh and the brief introductions of each of over 200 Noh Plays. It also contained several references of Noh books translated into foreign languages. I discovered for the first time the name of an English orientalist, Arthur Waley (1910 ～ 1966), and his book, "The Noh Plays of Japan" (TUTTLE PUBLISHING).The book offered complete translations of 19 Noh plays. Arthur Waley is well known as the authur of "The Tale of Genji", a famous English version of an ancient Japanese love story, "Genji Monogatari". Waley's Noh scripts translated into

の簡単な紹介がありましたが、その時はその重要性に気づかず、TUTTLE PUBLISHINGが出版した本を、Koboのlibraryで見つけたのはずっと後の事です。

　私は中年になってから始めた謡の趣味が嵩じて、リタイアの10年位前にサラリーマン上がりの能楽師範になり、その後京都の河村同門として活動してきました。その間の20年間に主として河村研究能において、20番の能のシテを舞う機会を得たのです。そこで私は能の実演者としての経験を生かした、平易で分かりやすい英訳スクリプトを作る事を考えた訳です。然しながら能本の原文そのものは難解で、日本人でも直ぐには理解が難しく、それが能が広く現代社会に受け入れられるための敷居を高くしている程です。ここに能楽専門出版社の「檜書店」から発行されている「対訳で楽しむ」能本のシリーズがあります。二人の著名な能楽研究者が交代で執筆して、現代語に逐訳された35曲が既に発行され、今後14曲が予定されています。私がシテを舞った20番中10番がこのシリーズに入っているので、この10番を対象にして、現代日本語を英語に逐訳することにしました。既に10番の英訳は完成していますが、紙幅の制約もありその中の5番に絞って本書を発行することにしました。曲目を絞るにあたって考慮したのは、各曲の主題を大別する「五番建て」**を意識したこと並びに前述の二つの英訳本で既訳の曲と出来るだけ重ならないことの二つです。

　巻末にこれまで述べた英訳能の一覧表を付しています。ご参照ください。

　この本では能楽を鑑賞しようとされる多くの英語圏の外国人の方々、並びに日本語と英語のバイリンガルの方々に、舞台上で演じられているストーリーを、出来るだけ正確に且つ分かりやすく伝えることを念頭に、能の実践者としての経験を踏まえて訳しています。又、能本の

English all have a simple and poetic sensibility that makes you feel like you are rhythmically reciting an *Utai. At the same time, I feel they contain a little bit too much of abstract expression.

The Hinoki Shoten booklet also had a rather short reference to the book,"The Noh Drama-Ten Plays from the Japanese", translated by the Japanese Classics Translation Committee of The Japan Society for the Promotion of Science. The book was supposed to be completely translated into English, but I didn't realize its importance at that time. I found the book published by Tuttle Publishing at the Kobo library quite a while after that.

I became a Noh instructor as something of a sequel to devoting myself to practicing Utai, which I started in middle-age. This was 10 years before my retirement. Since, I've been practicing Noh-related activities as a member of the Kawamura School in Kyoto. Through these activities, I've had the opportunities to perform 20 pieces of Noh as Shi-te (pronunced SHEE-tay), the protagonist of a Noh Play, mainly at training sessions at the Kawamura School. This is one of the reasons why it occurred to me that I could create simple and understandable Noh scripts, making use of my experiences as a real Noh performer. However, original Noh scripts are very difficult for contemporary people to understand, because of its ancient style of the language, that is even for native Japanese speakers. This I think partly creates a large barrier for most of people in terms of coming to fondly appreciate Noh plays.

I soon found a series of books called "Noh Text with Paginal Translation",published by Hinoki Shoten. These books are written separately by two famous Noh researchers in modern Japanese with paginal translation ; 35 pieces have already been published and 14 more are planned. 10 pieces among 20 in which I've performed in Shi-te role, exist in these 35 pieces. Thus, I decided to start creating English scripts of these 10 pieces. I've already completed these 10 pieces, but this time I'm going to publish just 5 of the10 due to space constraints. I've selected 5 pieces based on the following two points. First, I considered covering all five categories of Noh themes, called ** "Goban Date".

Second, I considered avoiding overlapping the two books above, as much as possible, when making the piece selection. Actually, I believe that the three pieces selected are the first translations of them

原文、現代語ならびに英訳の三つを対比させた編集となっているので、特にバイリンガルの方々には、一層能のストーリーの理解を深めていただけると自負しています。今後発行予定の檜書店の「対訳シリーズ」には、私がシテを舞った20番中の2番が含まれています。機会があればその英訳にも取り組み、翻訳済みの残りの5番と併せて改めて世に問いたいと思います。

　最後に、翻訳について助言を得た英語ネイティブの二人、米国人英語教師ブライアン・コネリー氏並びにカナダ女性詩人・著述編集者、タミー高橋氏に感謝します。

　京都河村家には裏表紙の舞台写真・小鍛冶の舞台写真、並びに同家蔵の多くの能面・舞扇（中啓）の写真についてご協力と掲載のお許しを頂きました。また文芸社出版企画部三宅・岩田両氏、並びに編集部片山氏には和英両文の対訳という変則的な出版について多大のご尽力を頂きました。ともに記して御礼を申し上げます。

* 「謡」：能の中で演者や地謡（コーラス）によって謡われる吟唱や台詞のこと
** 「五番建て」

　　：古来、能の興行は一日を通して五番が演じられ、その主題によって常に一定の順番で行われる習いであった。即ち初番は神的な物、2番は男性的な戦物、3番は女性的な恋愛物、4番は遊狂を含むその他の物、そして5番・最後には鬼の物という風に時分に応じて観客を飽きさせない構成にしていた。

in the world.

For your reference, at the end of this book I put a table listing all those English translations of Noh scripts.

I've created my translations with the intention that the scripts will help encourage many English-speaking foreigners and bilingual people to become interested in watching Noh plays, as well as to help them understand the plays more easily, so that they can follow the stories as they are being performed on stage. I've made my translations trying to make the best use of my experiences as a Noh performer. On each page, the reader can also make a comparison my English scripts to, modern Japanese versions and the original scripts in ancient Japanese. I believe this may deepen people's understanding of Noh plays, especially for those who are bilingual.

The planned series of books by Hinoki Shoten, include 2 more pieces among 20 for which I've performed the role of Shi-te. I'd like to try to create these English scripts as well, and publish them along with already written 5 pieces.

Finally, I'd like to mention kind assistance of two native English speakers; an American teacher, Mr. Brian Connelly and Canadian poet and writer/editor, Mrs .Tammy Takahashi.

The Kawamuras in Kyoto offered me help with many photo images, including the picture of the whole Kawamura theater, stage photos of Noh Kokaji, and many pictures of masks and fans that are part of the Kawamuras' private collection.

The Bungeisha Corporation staff, Mr. Miyake and Mr. Iwata in the publishing planning department and Mr. Katayama in the editorial department, both dedicated a great deal of time and energy toward publishing the book with its rather irregular structuring of pages due to the contrasting structures between Japanese and English.

I greatly appreciate all these contributions.

*Utai : songs and lines recited by actors or the chorus in Noh plays.
**Gobandate : back in olden times, 5 Noh plays were performed throughout the day in order to entertain people for amusement.
5 plays are always arranged in a patterned order, based on the theme of each play: the first is Gods, the second Men, the third Women, and the fourth about some other topic involving are madwomen, for example, and others; the last is Demons.

能舞台　　Noh Theater

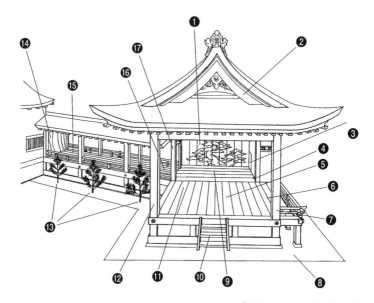

『対訳でたのしむ能』（檜書店）より転載
Reprinted from "Noh Text with Paginal Translation" (Hinoki Shoten)

❶鏡板；舞台背面にはめ込まれた板、老松が描かれている

❷屋根；能舞台が屋外に有った時の名残

❸切戸口；地謡や後見方の舞台への出入口

❹笛柱；笛方が近くに座る

❺舞台；約5.5m四方の板間、檜板が縦に張られている

❻地謡座；地謡方が座る位置

❼ワキ柱；ワキ方が常にこの柱の側に座る

❽白州；能舞台が屋外に有った時の名残、玉石が敷かれている

❶ *Kagami-ita*：the back wall with a pine- tree painted on it.

❷ *Roof*：based on the design of ancient Noh theaters, when they were located outdoors.

❸ *Kiridoguchi*：the door used by the chorus and the stage- attendant to exit and enter the stage.

❹ *Fuebashira*：the flute player's pillar.

❺ *Butai*：the stage; about 5.5-meter -square space, with hinoki cypress boards placed vertically.

❻ *Jiutaiza*：the place where the chorus members sit.

❼ *Wakibashira*：a pillar; the waki usually sits near it.

❽ *Shirasu*：based on the design of ancient Noh theaters, when they were located outdoors；pebbles are spread all over it.

❾後座：檜板が横に張られて
いる、向かって右から笛
方・小鼓方・大鼓方・太鼓
方が座り、左後方に後見方
が座る

❿階：舞台の開始を寺社奉行
が命じる時などに使用した
頃の名残

⓫常座：舞台に入ってきたシ
テが先ず足を止め、所作の
起点となる位置

⓬目付柱：能面を付け極度に
視野が狭められた演者の目
標となる柱

⓭舞台の方から一の松、二の
松、三の松

⓮揚幕：演者の出入りに際し、
二人の後見が竹竿で上げ下
げする

⓯橋掛り；演者が出入りする
通路、又舞台の延長として
の演技空間

⓰狂言座；間狂言が座り、控
えている所

⓱シテ柱；シテが常に立つ常
座の近くにある柱

❾ *Atoza*：a space with hinoki cypress boards placed horizontally; musicians for the flute, small drum, drum, and large drum sit here in order from right to left; the stage-attendant sits in the back left.

❿ *Kizahashi*：steps; based on the design of ancient Noh theaters, when authorities used the steps to order the start of the event.

⓫ *Jōza*：the Shi-te's seat; when the Shi-te enters the stage, he always stops here, to start his act.

⓬ *Metsuke-bashira*：pillar on which the actor fixes his eyes in order to ensure he is in the right position; the actor's vision is extremely limited from wearing the mask.

⓭ *Three pine-branches*：names from right to left： ichi no-matsu, ni no-matsu, san no-matsu.

⓮ *Agemaku*：curtain through which actors enter and exit the stage; two stage-attendants lift it with a bamboo stick as an actor's passes.

⓯ *Hashigakari*：the corridor through which actors access the stage; also an important extension of the stage itself.

⓰ *Kyōgenza*：the seat where the kyōgen-kata, who plays ai-kyōgen（a comedic intermission between Noh plays）, waits to perform.

⓱ *Shi-tebashira*：pillar located near the jōza, where the Shi-te usually stands.

凡　例

この本ではあらすじや各シーンの経過説明などが四角い囲みの中に書かれています。

このような囲みには能の台本の原文が書かれています。

こちらは
能の台本の現代語訳です

こちらは
能の台本の英訳です

Explanatory Notes

In this book, the outline, explanations of each scene and so on appear in a box like this.

The original Noh scripts appear in this box.

A translation into modern
Japanese appears here.

The English translated appears here.

高　砂
Takasago

能：初番物
Category: The First

P. 34　「掻けども落ち葉の尽きせぬは」
"Yet withered leaves are never depleted."

目　次

Contents

時は古今和歌集が勅命により編纂された延喜帝の時代、九州阿蘇神社の神主友成一行が都拝見に訪れる。旅の途中一行は名勝高砂の浦で老人夫婦（実は住吉明神の化身）に出会う。友成の問いに答えて二人は「相生の松」の謂れを語り、古の「万葉和歌集」と変わらず和歌の道が栄える今の延喜帝の御代を称える。

更に問われて老翁は和歌の道の繁栄と常盤の松のめでたさの謂れを語って曰く。

即ち和歌の功徳は自然界の草木をはじめ、陽の下の万物が皆和歌の心に染められる事によるのであり、殊に千年の樹齢を保つ常盤の松こそがめでたいのであると。

やがて老人夫婦は友成と住吉での再会を約し、海の彼方に姿を消す。友成一行は舟で後を追う。

住吉では住吉明神が若々しい姿を現し、祝福の舞を舞う。

能高砂は能楽が成立した室町時代から今日にいたるまで最も人気の高い代表的な祝言曲であり続けている。

中啓尉扇表

Jō fan（used for the elderly man）for Noh play -the front-

Outline

The time is the reign of Emperor Engi, when the anthology of poems, "Kokin Wakashū," is compiled by imperial command.

The Shinto priest, Tomonari, of Aso Shrine in Kyushu, and his entourage travel to visit the capital. On their way, they happen to meet a couple of elderly people, who are actually the embodiment of the Sumiyoshi Myōjin deities, at the scenic seashore in Takasago. Answering Tomonari's inquiry, the two of them tell him the tale of "Pine Trees, Aioi (Twin Pines) ," and also praise the ongoing reign of the Emperor Engi, when the waka poetry flourishes just as much as in the time of the ancient "Manyōshū."

Upon further inquiry, the elderly man tells the tale of poetry and the favorable auspices of the ever-green pine trees:The waka poetry thrives because all things under the sun, as well as the grasses and trees in nature, are imbued with poetic spirit, and the ever-green pine trees, which live for over a thousand years, are especially auspicious entities.

Then, the two elderly people agree with Tomonari to meet again in Sumiyoshi, and they disappear beyond the sea. Tomonari and his entourage follow them on a boat. Later, in Sumiyoshi, the Sumiyoshi Myōjin appears in a youthful form, and dances for blessings.

Takasago has been one of the most popular and representative auspicious Noh play from the Muromachi Period (1336-1573), when Noh originated, to present.

中啓尉扇裏

Same as on the left -the back-

注 記	
作 者	世阿弥
資 材	古今和歌集　仮名序（かなで書かれた序文）の記述に基づく
場 面	前場：春の夕暮れの高砂の浦（現兵庫県高砂市）
	後場：同日夜半の住吉神社（現大阪市住吉区）

登場人物		
名 前	役 柄	能 面
住吉に住む老翁	前シテ	子牛尉
住吉明神	後シテ	邯鄲男
姥 老翁の妻で高砂に住む	ツレ	姥（老女）
阿蘇友成	ワキ	無し
友成の従者	ワキツレ	無し
高砂の浦の男	アイ	無し

子牛尉
Koujijō

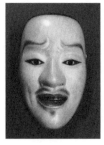
邯鄲男
Kantan man

姥
Uba

Notes	
Creator	Zeami
Materials	Based on the descriptions in the "Kokin Wakashu Kanajo" (introduction written in kana)
Scenes	The first half : A spring evening on the Takasago seashore (Takasago City, Hyogo Prefecture.)
	The second half : Sumiyoshi Shrine at night on the same day (Sumiyoshi Ward in Osaka City)

Characters		
Name	Role	Mask
An elderly man Living in Sumiyoshi	Shi-te in the first half	Koujijō
Sumiyoshi Myōjin (deity)	Shi-te in the second half	Kantan man
An elderly woman Elderly man's wife living in Takasago	Tsure	Uba (elderly woman)
Tomonari Aso	Waki	No mask
Tomonari's attendant	Wakitsure	No mask
A man living along the Takasago seashore	Ai	No mask

住吉明神
Sumiyoshi Myōjin (deity)

彼らは真ノ次第の囃子とともに幕より出で、橋掛かりを進んで舞台に入り、舞台中央に対面して立つ。

Scene 1 : Tomonari and his entourage appear, and discuss their long journey from their home port to their destination, Takasago.

They appear together from behind the curtain with the Shin no Shidai, played by Hayashi. They proceed down the corridor, enter the stage, and stand at center stage facing to each other.

［次第］

ワキワキツレ／今を始めの旅衣、今を始めの旅衣、日も行く末ぞ久しき。

［次第の謡　連吟］	[Shidai song：sung together]
友成一行（三度返し）：旅衣を身にまとい、旅衣を身にまとい、さあ遥かな遠旅に出立しよう。	Tomonari and his entourage (three time refrain)：Upon preparing travel outfits, upon preparing travel outfits, we'll start on our trip of a great distance.

［名ノリ］

ワキ／そもそもこれは九州肥後の国、阿蘇の宮の神主友成とは我が事なり、我いまだ都を見ず候程に、この度思ひ立ち都に上り候、又よき序なれば、播州高砂の浦をも一見せばやと存じ候。

［名ノリ］	[Self introduction]
友成：そもそも九州阿蘇神社の神主友成とは私のことです。私は未だ都を見たことがないので、このたびは訪ねようと思います。また、良い機会なので名高い播磨の高砂に立ち寄ることにします。	Tomonari：Well, I am the Shinto priest, Tomonari, of Aso shrine in Kyushu. I now wish to travel to see the capital, because I've never been there before. Also, we are stopping at the famous Takasago seashore in Harima province, on the way at our convenience.

ワキワキツレ／▽旅衣、末遥々の都路を、末遥々の都路を、今日思ひ立つ浦の波、船路のどけき春風の、幾日来ぬらん後末も。いさ白雲の遥々と、さしも思ひし播磨潟、高砂の浦に着きにけり、高砂の浦に着きにけり。

［道行の謡　連吟］

友成一行：旅衣を身にまとい、我らは都への遥かな道を、都への遥かな道を行く。我らが里を出て幾日過ぎただろうか。これまでは穏やかな舟旅だったが、あと如何ほどの長旅になるのだろうか。と思ううちにようやく播磨の国高砂の浦に到着した、ようやく播磨の国高砂の浦に到着した。

［着セリフ］友成は高砂の浦に到着した旨を述べ、一行は舞台右手前のワキ座に座る

[Traveling song : sung together]

Tomonari and his entourage：Upon wearing our travel outfits, we'll take our remote route to the capital, we'll take our remote route to the capital. We wonder how many days have passed, since we left our home port. We have had a peaceful voyage, but we don't know how much longer the journey will be. Then, we've at last arrived at Takasago seashore in Harima province, we've at last arrived at Takasago seashore in Harima province.

[Statement of arrival] Tomonari announces their arrival at the Takasago seashore. All of them sit on Wakiza, front stage right.

シーン2：老人夫婦の登場

老人夫婦（シテとツレ）が真ノ一声の囃子とともに幕より登場。まずツレが橋掛りを進み、右端にいったん止まり幕に向く。その間にシテが登場し、幕近くに止まり、橋掛りにて向き合う。やがて二人は一セイ、サシ、下歌、上歌の順に謡を謡う。これらの謡を通じて二人は、名所での静かな春の夕暮れの様と、そこでの長寿の暮らしぶりを述べる。このシーンの終わりに二人は舞台に入る。シテは熊手、ツレは箒を担げる。二人は神職の下僕の出立である。

Scene 2 : An elderly couple appear.

The elderly couple (Shi-te and Tsure) appear from behind the curtain with Shin no Issei music by Hayashi. First, Tsure proceeds down the corridor, stops at the end of it, and turns toward the curtain. While Tsure proceeding, Shi-te appears and stops near the curtain, so that they are standing in the corridor facing each other. Then, they sing the Issei song, Sashi song, downtone song, and uptone song, in that order. Through all these songs, they talk about the calmness of the spring evening at the scenic site and how to live a longevity life. At the end of the scene, they enter the stage. Shi-te holds a rake, and Tsure holds a broom. Both wear the outfit of the under servant for Shinto priests.

[一セイ]

シテツレ／高砂の、松の春風吹き暮れて、尾上の鐘も響くなり。

[一セイの謡　連吟]

老人夫婦：高砂の松を春風が吹きわたり、夕暮れには山上から鐘の音をここまで運んでくる。

[Issei song : sung together]

The elderly couple：Here in Takasago, a spring breeze is blowing through the pine trees, and it conveys the sound of the bell from the mountaintop all the way to the seashore in the evening.

ツレ／波は霞の磯がくれ、

姥：春霞に隠れて磯の波は見えないが……

The elderly woman：Although we can't see the wave along the beach because of the spring haze,

シテツレ／音こそ汐の満干なれ。

老人夫婦：波音が近づくので、汐の満ちるのがわかる。

The couple：We know there is a flood tide thanks to the approaching sounds.

[サシ]
シテ／誰をかも知る人にせん高砂の。松も昔の友ならで、

[サシの謡]
姥：和歌の詠に言う：高砂の松よりずっと年を経てきたので、古の事どもを他の誰に話してよいものやら。

[Sashi song]
The elderly woman：The poem says：I've become so older than the pine trees in Takasago that I don't know, to whom I can talk about the ancient matters, other than them.

シテツレ／過ぎ来し世々は白雪の、積り積りて老の鶴の、塒に残る有明の、春の霜夜の起居にも、松風をのみ聞き馴れて、心を友と菅筵の、思ひを延ぶるばかりなり。

老人夫婦：我らはこれまで幾星霜を重ねてきたのか。髪は積もり積もった雪か、はたまた千年の年を経た鶴の如くに白髪となった。春の霜夜の暁や有明の月が残る朝には早起きをし、ただ松に吹く静かな風の音のみを聞き、我らはただ風雅の心、和歌に感動を託するばかりの日々を送っている。

The couple：We wonder how long we have been getting older. Our hair has become white, like piled up snow or cranes that have grown by a thousand years. We often get up early in the morning, when it's frosty dawn in the spring, and the waning moon lingers in the morning sky. We always only listen to the serene sounds of the wind through pine trees, and live our daily lives with our refined tastes of heart, these hearts that are only moved by poems.

［下歌］

シテツレ／\ 訪（おとづ）れは、松に言問（ことと）ふ浦風（うらか）の、落葉衣（おちばごろも）の袖添（そでそ）へて、木蔭（こかげ）の塵（ちり）を掻（か）かうよ、木蔭（こかげ）の塵（ちり）を掻（かお）かうよ。

［下歌の謡］

同人たち：誰かの訪れを待っても、海から松に吹く風の訪ればかり。その浦風が松の葉を吹き落とし、我らが袖に落ちかかる。その我らが袖に箒を持ち、木陰の落葉を掃き清めよう。

[Sing downtone]

The couple：We are expecting someone to visit us, but all we have is the wind from the sea blowing through the pine trees. The wind from the sea blows down the leaves of the pine trees, so that they fall upon our sleeves. With our sleeves, we are holding our broom, and we're sweeping and cleaning the withered leaves.

［上歌］

シテツレ／\ 所は高砂（たかさご）の、所は高砂の、尾上（おのえ）の松も年ふりて、老（おい）の波も寄（よ）り来（く）るや、木の下蔭（したかげ）の落葉（おち）かく、なるまで命（いのち）ながらへて。なほ何時（いつ）までか生（おい）の松、それも久しき名所（めいしょ）かな、それも久しき名所かな。

［上歌の謡］

同人たち：所は高砂の、所は高砂の名高い尾上の松も我らとともに年を経た。寄る年波は岸に寄せる波に似て、ひたひたと迫る。木の下影の落葉を掃き集めるうち、ともに命を長らえたことだ。さらにいつまででこの松諸共生きながらえることになるのか。そうだ、あの名高い「生きの松」というのも昔から九州にはあったなあ。

[Sing uptone]

The same：Here in Takasago, here in Takasago, the famous pine tree of Onoe has gotten as old as we have. Our age sneaks up upon us, much like the waves that lap against the shore, only to retreat, and edge back again and again. Both enjoy longevity as we are sweeping and gathering the withered leaves. How much longer will we live, together with this pine tree? Well, I now remember the famous "Iki no Matsu (living pine tree)" (＊Iki means living in Japanese) in Kyushu, the famous "Iki no Matsu" in Kyushu.

友成の問いかけに老人夫婦は高砂と住吉の相生の松の謂れを物語る。

Scene 3 : Dialogue between Tomonari and the elderly couple.

Upon being asked by Tomonari, the couple relate the episode of the twin-pine trees, in Takasago and Sumiyoshi.

ワキ／里人を相待つ処に、老人夫婦来れり、いかにこれなる老人に尋ぬべき事の候。

友成：里人との出会いを待っ
ていると、老人夫婦がお見え
になった。申し、お二人にお
尋ねしたいことがあります。

Tomonari : While waiting to meet some villagers, I can see an elderly couple down there. Hello, I have something to ask you, the elderly.

シテ／此方の事にて候か何事にて候ぞ。

老翁：私どものことでしょう
か。お尋ねとは何事でしょう？

Elderly man : You're asking me. What's that?

ワキ／高砂の松とは何れの木を申し候ぞ。

友成：高砂の松とは、どの松
のことでしょうか？

Tomonari : Which tree do they call the Takasago-pine tree?

シテ／只今木蔭を清め候こそ高砂の松にて候へ。

老翁：我らが木陰を掃き清め
ている松こそ、それです。

Elderly man : It's the one under which we are sweeping and cleaning.

ワキ／高砂住吉の松に相生の名あり、当所と住吉とは国を隔てたるに、何とて相生の松とは申し候ぞ。

友成：高砂の松、住吉の松は相生の松と言われています。播磨の国高砂と摂津の国住吉とは国を隔てていますのに、何故相生の松と言われるのでしょう？

Tomonari：They say that the Takasago-pine tree and Sumiyoshi- pine tree are twin- trees (called Aioi). Why do they call these trees twin- pine trees (Aioi pine trees), in spite of Takasago in Harima and Sumiyoshi in Settsu belonging to different provinces?

シテ／仰せの如く古今（コキン）の序（ジョ）に、高砂住吉の松も、相生のやうに覚え（オボ）とありさりながら、この尉（ジョオ）は津の国住吉（スミヨシ）の者、これなる姥（ンバ）こそ当所（トオショ）の人なれ、知る事あらば申（エ）さ給へ。

老翁：おっしゃるとおり、古今和歌集の仮名序では、高砂、住吉の松は同じ一つの根から分かれて生え育ったとあります。ところで、私は摂津の国住吉出身の者、あの姥こそ、この播磨の国高砂に住む者です。
（姥に向かい）其方も何か知っていることがあればお話ししなさい。

Elderly man：As you talk, Kokin Wakashu Kanajo (introduction written by Kana) says "Takasago-pine tree and Sumiyoshi- pine tree seem to be twins that grew separately from the same root". By the way, I'm from Sumiyoshi in Settsu Province, and this elderly woman lives here in Takasago, in this Harima Province.
(Toward her) Why don't you talk to anything you know about these things?

ワキ／不思議や見れば老人（ロオジン）の、夫婦一所（イツショ）にありながら、遠き住吉高砂（スミノエ）の、浦山国（ウラヤマクニ）を隔てて（ヘダ）住むと、云ふ（イウ）は如何（イカ）なる事やらん、

友成：不思議なことだ。お二人は夫婦一緒でありながら、遠く海山を隔てた高砂と住吉とに分かれて住むというのは如何したことだ。

Tomonari：It's a strange thing that these elderly people are said to live separately in different provinces, Sumiyoshi and Takasago which are isolated from each other by mountains and seashores, in spite of them being married couple.

ツレ／うたての仰せ候や、山川万里を隔つれども、互に通ふ心遣ひの、妹背の道は遠からず、

姥：つまらないことをおっしゃいますな。遠く海山を隔てて分かれて住むと言っても、互いに心が通じている夫婦は親密な間柄を保てるのです。	Elderly woman：You are saying a paltry thing. Even if they actually live separately in different provinces that are isolated by mountains and seashores, a couple who can sympathize with each other, can form intimate relationships.

シテ／まづ案じても御覧ぜよ、

老翁：まずは考えてみてください。	Elderly man：Why don't you think about these things?

シテツレ／高砂住吉の、松は非情の物だにも、相生の名はあるぞかし、ましてや生ある人として、年久しくも住吉より、通ひ馴れたる尉と姥は、松もろともにこの年まで、相生の夫婦となるものを。

老人夫婦：高砂、住吉の松には「相生」の名があり、それは非情のものであるのに、ともに生きることを意味しています。ましてや我らは情を備えた生き物であり、永年夫婦として通っているのです。今や私どもは、ともに生きる夫婦になっているのです。	The couple：The Takasago and Suminoe pine trees have the name, "Aioi", which means co-exist, in spite of them are just plants without emotion. Moreover, we are living things with emotion, and I've been traveling far to meet her for many long years. We have now become a co-existing married couple.

ワキ／謂はれを聞けば面白や、さてさて前に聞えつる、相生の松の物語を、所に言ひ置く謂はれはなきか、

友成：謂れを聞けば面白いことですね。さてさて先程お聞きした相生の松について、何かご当地で昔から言い伝えられてきたことはありますか？

Tomonari：I'm very interested in what you're saying. Well then, is there any story about the twin- pine trees I've heard before, that has been handed down from a long time ago?

シテ／昔の人の申ししは、これはめでたき世の例（タメシ）なり、

老翁：昔の人の話では、これは素晴らしいご治世を喩えたものだとか。

Elderly man：Ancient people say that this turns to allegory the greatness of the reign.

ツレ／高砂と云ふは上代（イウ ジョオダイ）の、万葉集（マンニョオシウ）の古（イニシエ）の義（ぎ）、

姥：高砂というのは万葉和歌集が編纂された古代のご治世のこと。

Elderly woman："Takasago" means the ancient reign, when "Mannyo Wakashu" was compiled.

シテ／住吉（スミヨシ）と申すは、今この御代（ミヨ）に住み給ふ延喜（オ エンギ）の御事（オン）、

老翁：住吉というのは今の「延喜」のご治世、すなわち醍醐帝の御事。

Elderly man："Sumiyoshi" means the reigning sovereign "Engi", Emperor Daigo.

ツレ／松とは尽きぬ言（コト）の葉（ハ）の、

姥：「松」とは、とこしえに栄える和歌の道の意。

Elderly woman："Pine Tree" is a term of the art of Tanka poetry, symbolizing eternal prosperity.

シテ／栄えは古今相同（コ コンアイオナ）じと、

老翁：和歌の道は「万葉」の

Elderly man：The art of Tanka poetry has

昔も今の「古今」も同じ栄
と、

retained its prosperity from the ancient
"Mannyo" to today's "Kokin".

シテツレ／御代を崇むる喩へなり、

老人夫婦：これらはすべて素
晴らしいご治世の喩えなのです。

The couple：These things turn to allegory
the greatness of the reign.

ワキ／よくよく聞けばありがたや、今こそ不審春の日の、

友成：お聞きして嬉しいこと
です。これですっかり疑問が
晴れました。折から春の夕日
が照り染めて。

Tomonari：I'm very glad to hear that, and
all my queries have become clear to me.
Now, the evening sunlight in the spring is
shining.

シテ／光和らぐ西の海の、

老翁：西ノ海から穏やかな日
差しが降り注ぎ、

Elderly man：The peaceful sunlight is
shining from the western sea.

ワキ／彼処は住吉、

友成：彼処は住吉、

Tomonari：There is Suminoe province.

シテ／此処は高砂、

老翁：此処は高砂の浦、

Elderly man：Here is the Takasago seashore.

ワキ／松も色添ひ、

友成：名高い松も緑を増し、

Tomonari：The famous pine trees have
become greener.

シテ／春も、

老翁：春も、 | Elderly man：The spring is

ワキ／長閑（ノドカ）に、

友成：長閑に、 | Tomonari：Peaceful.

［上歌］
地／四海波静かにて、国も治まる時つ風、枝（エダ）を鳴らさぬ御代（ミヨ）なれや、あひに相生（イ　アイオイ）の、松こそめでたかりけれ。げにや仰（アオ）ぎても、事も疎（オロ）かやかかる代（ヨ）に、住める民とて豊（ユタ）かなる、君の恵（メグ）みぞありがたき、君の恵みぞありがたき。

［上歌の謡］
地謡：我が国を取り囲む四海は波も穏やかで静か、折から吹く風さえも枝葉を揺らすことはない。この素晴らしいご治世に相生の松に出会える幸運を喜び、この御代に生きることを限りなく有難く思う。わが君のおかげで豊かに生きている。君の恵みのなんと有難いことだ、君の恵みのなんと有難いことだ。

[Sing uptone]
Chorus：The sea surrounding this country now seems to be calm and quiet, and the reign is retaining its peace. Not even a fitful wind will be able to stir the leaves. In this great reign, we are fortunate to see the twin-pine trees. We are supremely thankful to be living in this great reign. We can live in immense prosperity thanks to our lord. How thankful we are for our lord's blessing, how thankful we are for our lord's blessing.

シーン４：老翁の物語

友成の要請を受け、老翁は齢千年の松のめでたさになぞらえて、和歌の道の祝福を物語る。自然界の万物はその立てる物音までもが和歌の美しさの表現となるものである。老翁続けて曰く、草木は四季の移り変わりをよく知り、人の心を持つかのようである。万木の中にあって松こそは最も高貴な徳を備え、永遠の和歌の道に喩えられる。かくて老翁は語り終え、この相生の松はとりわけめでたいと結ぶ。クリの謡の直前に老翁は常座から舞台中央に進み、着座する。ツレの姥も老翁の後ろに座る。クセの謡の後半、シテは立ち落葉を掻く所作をする。

Scene 4 : The elderly man tallks.

Upon Tomonari's request, the elderly man is relating auspiciousness of the art of Tanka poetry, referring to a similar auspicious thousand year- old pine tree. Everything in Nature embodies the art of beauty in Tanka poetry, even through the making of sound. The elderly man continues : The grass and trees well know the four seasonal changes, and seem to have human-like hearts. Among all the trees, the pine trees have the most noble integrity, as they turn allegory into eternal art of Tanka poetry affirming auspiciousness of these twin- pine trees. Right before the Kuri song, he proceeds from the Johza to center stage, and sits there. Tsure, the elderly woman, sits behind him too. At latter half of the Kuse song, Shi-te stands up and makes a gesture of sweeping the withered leaves.

ワキ／なほなほ高砂の松のめでたき謂はれ委しく御物語り候へ。

友成：高砂の松がそれほどめでたい謂れをもっと教えてください。

Tomonari : Please tell me more about why the Takasago tree is so auspicious.

［クリ］
地／それ草木心なしとは申せども花実の時を違へず、陽春の徳を具へて南枝花始めて開く。

[クリの謡]

地謡：さてさて草木は生命も感情も持たず、非情のものというが、花を咲かせ実を結ぶ時季は過たない。暖かな陽春を受けて、まず南側の枝から花を開き始める。

[Kuri song]

Chorus：Well then, the grass and trees are said to be an inanimate object without life or sympathy, but they don't mistake the time of their blooming and bear fruit. Upon being bathed in warm spring sunlight, the south side branches of the tree first starts to bloom.

[サシ]

シテ／然れどもこの松は、その気色（ケシキ）とこしなへ（エ）にして花葉（クワヨオ）時を分（ワ）かず、

[サシの謡]

老翁：一方でこの松というものは、いつも外観が変わらず、かつ、花が散り葉を落とすということがありません。

[Sashi song]

Elderly man：On the other hand, the pine trees always show the same outer appearances, and they don't scatter their flowers ; nor do their leaves fall.

地／四つの時至りても、一千年（イッセンネン）の色（イロ）雪の中（ウチ）に深く、また松花（ショオクワ）の色十廻（トカエ）りとも言（イ）へ（エ）り、

地謡：四季の終わりに冬となっても葉はいよいよ緑が濃くなり、雪に映えて色深くなります。しかし、また千年に一度花が咲き、それを十度繰り返すとも言われています。

Chorus：Even in the winter, at the end of the four seasons, their leaves get greener and are brightly colored in the white snow. Well then, they are supposed to bloom once every thousand years, and this repeats 10 times.

シテ／かかるたよりを松が枝（エ）の、

老翁：このような繰り返しを永遠ともいえるほど繰り返す松のめでたさのように、

Elderly man：How auspicious that they repeat this blooming cycle, so as to seem almost eternal.

地／言の葉草の露の玉、心を磨く種となりて、

地謡：同じくめでたく、素晴らしく美しい和歌の言葉が、古より今日まで続いてきて、人々の歌心を進める縁となって……

Chorus：Similarly auspicious, the fine verse of Tanka poetry has lasted from ancient times to today, and it encourages people to compose more poems.

シテ／生きとし生けるものごとに、

老翁：生きとし生けるものはすべて、

Elderly man：So, they say that all the living things have…

地／敷島のかげに寄るとかや。

地謡：「敷島の道」（日本古来の和歌の道）とも呼ばれる和歌の道に心を寄せ、また、歌を詠むのである。

Chorus：…empathy with the art of Tanka poetry, also called "Shikishima no Michi (the art of classical Japanese poetry)" and compose Tanka poetry.

［クセ］

地／然るに、長能が詞にも、有情非情のその声、みな歌に洩るる事なし、草木土砂、風声水音まで、万物の籠む心あり。春の林の、東風に動き秋の虫の、北露に鳴くも、皆和歌の姿ならずや。中にもこの松は、万木に勝れて、十八公のよそほひ、千秋の緑をなして、古今の色を見ず、始皇の御爵に、預かる程の木なりとて、異国にも、本朝にも、万民これを賞翫す。

［クセの謡］

地謡：さて藤原長能が書いた和歌の道の本にも言う：生き物か否かを問わず、その発する声や音はすべからく歌となるものである。思うに、草

[Kuse song]

Chorus：Well then, the book on the art of Tanka poetry, written by Nagatoh Fujiwara, says that any voice or sound can be poetic, regardless of whether they come from living things or inanimate things. We can

木、土砂、風の声、水の流れに至るまで、この世のすべてのものには歌の心が籠っている。また、春の林が東風に葉を鳴らし、秋の虫が露に濡れて鳴くのも、すべて和歌の心そのものではないか、と。なかでもこの松というのは最も徳が高く、その漢字を分解して十八公と読まれるほどに風格があり、また、千年の緑を保ちうるのである。松は秦の始皇帝から爵位を賜る栄誉に浴している。よって我が国でも中国でも、すべての人に愛で慈しまれているのである。

extrapolate from this that everything in this world, including the grass, trees, soil, sand, and the sound of the wind and streams, contains the art of poetry. It is also said that is all the art of Tanka poetry itself, that the spring wind from the east stirs the leaves in the forest, and insects are chirping, wet with autumn dewdrops. Among all kind of trees, the pine tree is the most virtuous, as noble as its Chinese Character ; the three parts comprising it mean the eighteen dukes, and are able to remain green for thousand years. They have even had a noble title bestowed on them by The first Qin Emperor in China. Then everybody, both in our country and in China, praises and loves this great tree.

シテ／高砂の、尾上(オノエ)の鐘(カネ)の音すなり、

老翁：高砂の山上から鐘の音が聞こえてくる。

Elderly man：Here is the sound of the bell ringing on the mountaintop of Takasago.

地／ 暁(アカツキ) かけて、霜(シモ)は置けども松が枝の、葉色は同じ深緑(フカミドリ)、立ち寄る蔭(カゲ)の朝夕(アサイウ)に、掻けども落葉(オチバ)の尽きせぬは、真(マコト)なり松の葉の、散り失せずして色はなほ、真(マ)折(サキ)の葛(カヅラ)ながき世の、喩(タト)へ(エ)なりける常盤木(トキワギ)の、中(ナカ)にも名は高砂の、末代(マツダイ)の例(タメシ)にも、相生の松ぞめでたき。

地謡：明け方に霜が降りたようだ。霜が降りると山寺の鐘の音を響かせると言われる。歌にも詠まれるように、たとえ霜が降りても高砂の松の葉

Chorus：There may have been frost at dawn ; it's said that the frost allows for the mountain temple bells to sound. There's a poem that says that even if it has frosted over, the leaves of the Takasago pine tree will

は緑を失わないのである。我らが朝に夕に木の下の落葉を、掻いても、掻いてもそれが尽きることがない。まさに「古今集仮名序」に言うとおり、松の葉は散り失せることなく木はとこしえの緑を保つのである。これぞ素晴らしいご治世同様に和歌の喩えとなる常緑の木であり、なかでも高砂の松は名高い相生の松としてとこしえの祝福を顕している。

still remain green. We sweep and clean the fallen leaves under the tree every morning and evening, yet withered leaves are never depleted. Exactly like the phrases from "Kokinshu Kanajo" say, the leaves of the pine tree are never depleted in falling, and remain forever green. This is the evergreen tree, an allegory for Tanka poetry, as well as the great reign. The Takasago pine tree is especially famous twin-tree, that will forever be auspicious.

シーン5：老人夫婦の中入り

老人夫婦の話を聞き、友成は二人が只者でないと気づき、本体を顕すよう願う。二人は自らを相生の松の精、すなわち住吉明神と名乗り、住吉で会おうと言い、舟に乗って沖の彼方に姿を消す。

Scene 5 : The elderly couple withdraw. (intermission)
Upon hearing the elderly couple's talk, Tomonari realizes their extraordinaire, and ask them reveal their real identity. The couple introduces themselves as the twin-pine tree's spirits, the Sumiyoshi God, tells him to meet at Sumiyoshi, and disappears beyond the sea on the boat.

[ロンギ]

地／げに名を得たる松が枝(エ)の、げに名を得たる松が枝(エ)の、老木(オイキ)の昔顕(アラワ)して、その名を名のり給へや、

[ロンギの謡]

地謡：どうか名高い松の木のようなそのご老体の本当のお

[Rongi song]

Chorus：Please reveal your real identity of the elderly things like the famous pine tree,

姿を顕して、真のお名前をお明かしください。	and tell me your real name.

シテツレ／今は何をか裏（ツツ）むべき、これは高砂住吉（スミノエ）の、相生の松の精（セイ）、夫婦と現（ゲン）じ来りたり、

老人夫婦：今は何を隠しましょう。我らは高砂と住吉の相生の松の精であり、夫婦の姿となって現れたのです。	Elderly couple：We will now tell the truth. We are the twin- pine tree's spirits, Takasago and Sumiyoshi, appearing as the figure of couple.

地／不思議やさては名所（ナドコロ）の、松の奇特（キドク）を顕（アラワ）して、

地謡：なんと不思議なことだ。さてはこれは名高い松の木が奇跡を示されたのですか？	Chorus：What a wonder this is. Well, is this a miracle on account of the famous pine tree?

シテツレ／草木（ソウモク）心なけれども、

老人夫婦：草木は感情を示さない非情のものであるけれども……	Elderly couple：The grass and trees are inanimate things without emotion, but…

地／畏（カシコ）き代（ヨ）とて、

地謡：この素晴らしいご治世なので……	Chorus：… now in this great reign,…

シテツレ／土も木も、

老人夫婦：土も木もすべてのものは…	Elderly couple：…the soil, trees and every other thing are…

地／我が大君の国なれば、何時までも君が代に、住吉に先づ行きて、あれにて待ち申さんと、夕波の汀なる、海士の小舟にうち乗りて、追風に任せつつ、沖の方に出でにけりや、沖の方に出でにけり。

地謡：我らが帝が治められる国土の一部であり、我らもそのご治世にいつまでも住みたいとここに姿を顕しました。我らは先に住吉に赴き、そこで貴方様をお待ちします。と二人は言い置き、漁夫の舟に乗って追い風に吹かれるまま沖の彼方へ行ってしまった。

Chorus：…the part of our country that our Majesty is reigning over. So we appear here, hoping to live eternally in the reign. We are going ahead of you to Sumiyoshi, and will see you again there. The couple spoke thus, and then went beyond the sea, have gone beyond the sea, onto the fisherman's boat, swaying in the fair wind.

友成は従者に命じて浦の者（アイ）を呼び出させる。アイは橋掛りの右端の狂言座に控えている。呼び出しを受けてアイは舞台中央に着座し、友成の問いに答えて話す。すなわち、相生の松は和歌の繁栄の象徴であり、高砂、住吉の両明神は夫婦の間柄であると。そしてアイは、老人夫婦は恐らく両明神であろうと教え、新造の舟への乗船を促し、追い風に乗って出立するように勧める。（この対話そのものはここには記載されない）

Scene 6 : Aikyōgen's talk. (an explanatory interlude between the two halves of a Noh play performed by Kyōgen-kata, comedic performers in Noh.)

Tomonari asks one member of his entourage to call the villager (Ai), who is sitting in Aiza, which is located at the right end of the corridor. Ai sits center stage, and is answering Tomonari's queries. He relates that the twin-pine tree is the symbol of prosperity in Tanka poetry, and that the two gods, Takasago and Sumiyoshi are spouses. Then, he points out that the elderly couple may be the two gods, asks them to board on the newly made boat, and urges them to sail sea in the fair wind. (the dialogue itself isn't written on the text)

シーン7：友成の待謡

アイが退場すると友成一行が舞台中央に進み待謡を謡う。一行が高砂を出立し、住吉に到着する意である。

Scene 7 : Tomonari sings the Machiutai (waiting song).

Tomonari and his entourage enter the center stage, right after Ai withdraws, and sing the Machiutai, which says that they are leaving Takasago seashore and arriving at Sumiyoshi.

［待謡］

ワキ　ワキツレ／＼高砂や、この浦船（ウラブネ）に帆（ホ）をあげて、この浦船に帆をあげて、月もろともに出汐（イデシオ）の、波の淡路（アワヂ）の島影（シマカゲ）や、遠く鳴尾（ナルヲ）の沖（オキ）過ぎて、はや住吉（スミノエ）に着きにけり、はや住吉（スミノエ）に着きにけり。

[待謡の謡　連吟]
友成一行：高砂の浦に帆を揚げて、高砂の浦に帆を揚げて、月の出とともに上げ潮に乗って出航した。波のかなたに淡路の島影を望み、鳴尾の沖を過ぎて、早や住吉潟に到着した、早や住吉潟に到着した。

[Machiutai song：sung together]
Tomonari and his entourage：Putting up a sail at Takasago seashore, putting up a sail at Takasago seashore, we left the port at high tide, accompanied by the rise of the moon. Then we saw Awaji island beyond the waves, and sailed past Naruo inlet. Now we have just arrived at Sumiyoshi bay, we have just arrived at Sumiyoshi bay.

シーン8：住吉明神（後シテ）の登場

住吉明神が出端の囃子にのって幕から勢いよく登場。橋掛りーの松（舞台側）に止まり、サシの謡（和歌の朗唱）を謡う。

Scene 8：The Sumiyoshi god (Shi-te in the second half) appears.
The Sumiyoshi god appears dashingly from behind the curtain, accompanied by Deha music, played by Hayashi. He stops at Ichinomatsu (near the stage) along the corridor and sing the Sashi song (referring to Tanka poetry).

[サシ]
後シテ／我見ても久しくなりぬ住吉（スミヨシ）の、岸（キシ）の姫松（ヒメマツ）幾代（イク ヨ）経（へ）ぬらん、睦ましと君は知らずや瑞籬（ミヅガキ）の、久しき代々（ヨ）の神（カミ）かぐら、夜（ヨル）の鼓（ツヅミ）の拍子（ヒョオシ）を揃（ソロ）へて、すずしめ給へ（エ）宮（ミヤ）つ子たち。

[サシの謡]
住吉明神：初めて見てから幾星霜を経ただろうか。ここ住吉の浦の美しい松は幾世代を経た古木なのだろうか？　わが君はわれがこの松と睦ましく、君を寿ぐことをご存知だろう

[Sashi song]
Sumiyoshi god："A long time has passed since I saw it for the first time. How many years have the fine pine trees been growing here in Sumiyoshi seashore?" "Doesn't our Majesty know that I've been in a close relationship with them in order to celebrate

か？　このように神々が詠み交わされた和歌に言うように、神官たちよ、古来捧げてきた素晴らしい拍子の神楽をもって神々を鎮め申し上げよ。

you?" Thus, the gods exchanged their Tanka poetry. Like this, please quiet the gods with the sacred music in fine rhythm, with which you Shinto priests have been serving the gods since ancient times.

シーン9：住吉明神（後シテ）の舞

後シテが舞台に入り、自らを名乗り千年の緑を保つ松と早春の梅の花の美しさを称え、神舞を舞う。

Scene 9 : The Sumiyoshi god (Shi-te in the second half) dances.

He enters the stage, introduces himself, describes the beauty of the thousand-year longevity and greenness of pine trees, as well as the plum blossoms in early spring, and then dances the Kamimai.

地／⌒西の海、檍が原の波間より。

地謡：西の海、檍が原の波間より……

Chorus : From the waves of the western sea, Aokigahara…

シテ／⌒現れ出でし神松の。

住吉明神：われは和歌に詠まれた如くに出現する。すなわち、西の海のかなた、日向の国檍が原の波間より生まれ出たのがわれ住吉明神である（檍が原では古の伊弉諾尊が禊をされた）。

Sumiyoshi god : …I'm appearing like the Tanka poetry says ; It's me, the Sumiyoshi god that was born among the waves of the western sea, Aokigahara in Hyuga province (where a holy ancient god named Izanagi performed the purification ceremony).

シテ／⌒春なれや、残んの雪の浅香潟、

同人：春にはここ住吉の浅香潟では残りの雪のみが見える。

The same：In the spring, all that can be seen is the remaining snow here in the Asaka inlet in Sumiyoshi.

地／〽玉藻刈るなる岸蔭の、

地謡：松の繁る浅香潟の岸辺では人々が玉藻を刈り……

Chorus：There are pine trees on the shores of Asaka inlet, where people reap "Tamamo", or algae.

シテ／〽松根に倚って腰を摩れば、

住吉明神：われはその松の根方に座り、その長寿に肖ろうと腰を擦れば……

Sumiyoshi god：I'm sitting on the root of a long-living pine tree, and rubbing against it in order to be blessed with longevity…

地／〽千年の翠手に満てり。

地謡：千年続く緑がわが手に満ち溢れる。

Chorus：…My hands are full with the greenness that lasts a thousand-years.

シテ／〽梅花を折つて頭に挿せば、

住吉明神：梅の枝を折って頭に挿せば……

Sumiyoshi god：Upon holding the plum blossoms up over my head…

地／〽二月の雪衣に落つ。

地謡：花びらが早春の雪のように、わが衣に降りかかる。

Chorus：…the petals are fluttering upon my clothes like the snow in early spring.

<table>
<tr>
<td>

神舞（急調の舞）

住吉明神は笛、小鼓、大鼓、太鼓のみによって奏される囃子に乗って舞を舞う。

</td>
<td>

Kamimai (up tempo dancing)

The Sumiyoshi god dances the Kamimai, accompanied by a hayashi : played by flute, small drum, drum and big drum, without any songs.

</td>
</tr>
</table>

シーン10：結末

住吉明神は数々の舞楽の名を上げながら舞台を巡り、人々が平安を謳歌する御代を寿ぎ、謡い舞う。

Scene 10 : Ending

The Sumiyoshi god has chosen several kinds of dance, dances around the stage while singing, and gives high praise to the reign, where the people can live in peace.

[ロンギ]

地／ありがたの影向（ヨオゴオ）や、ありがたの影向や、月住吉（スミヨシ）の神遊（カミアソビ）、御影（ミカゲ）を拝むあらたさよ、

[ロンギの謡]	[Rongi song]
地謡：有難い神のご降臨よ、有難い神のご降臨よ。月に照らされ、ここ住吉で神楽を聴き、神の御姿を拝む有難さよ。	Chorus：How thankful we are that the god is coming, how thankful we are that the god is coming. We are so pleased to be able to see the sacred god's figure, here in Sumiyoshi under the moonlight, while hearing the sacred music.

シテ／げにさまさまの舞姫（マイヒメ）の、声も澄（ス）むなり住吉（スミノエ）の、松影（マツカゲ）も映（ウツ）るなる、青海波（セイガイハ）とはこれやらん、

住吉明神：ここ住吉では様々の舞姫の澄んだ歌声がはっきりと聞こえ、松の木の緑が青	Sumiyoshi god：The singing voices of many dancing ladies' can be clearly heard here in Sumiyoshi, and the greenness of pine trees is

海に照り映える。「青海波（青海の波）」とはこのことか？

reflecting upon the blue water. Is this the piece of music, "Seigaiha (waves of the blue water)"?

地／<ruby>神<rt>カミ</rt></ruby>と君との道すぐに、都の春に行くべくは、

地謡：わが君のご治世の如くに神慮に叶い、まっすぐに春満開の都に行こうとするならば……

Chorus：If you are going to the capital in the full bloom of the spring, as directly and powerfully as our majesty's reign is,…

シテ／それぞ<ruby>還城楽<rt>ゲンジョオラク</rt></ruby>の舞、

住吉明神：それこそ「都に帰る」という意味の「還城楽」の舞。

Sumiyoshi god：…That's nothing if not the music of "Genjouraku", which means "returning the capital."

地／さて<ruby>萬歳<rt>バンゼイ</rt></ruby>の、

地謡：さて君万歳と祈りを込め……

Chorus：Well then, we are praying sincerely.

シテ／<ruby>小忌衣<rt>コ ミ ゴロモ</rt></ruby>、

住吉明神：斎清めた衣を纏い。

Sumiyoshi god：I'm wearing my sacred clothes,

地／さす<ruby>腕<rt>カイナ</rt></ruby>には、<ruby>悪魔<rt>アクマ</rt></ruby>を<ruby>払<rt>ハラ</rt></ruby>ひ、をさむる手には、<ruby>寿福<rt>ジュフク</rt></ruby>を<ruby>抱<rt>イダ</rt></ruby>き、<ruby>千秋楽<rt>センシウラク</rt></ruby>は民を<ruby>撫<rt>ナ</rt></ruby>で、<ruby>萬歳楽<rt>マンザイラク</rt></ruby>には<ruby>命<rt>イノチ</rt></ruby>を<ruby>延<rt>ノ</rt></ruby>ぶ、相生の<ruby>松風<rt>マツ</rt></ruby>、<ruby>颯々<rt>サツ</rt></ruby>の声ぞ<ruby>楽<rt>タノ</rt></ruby>しむ、颯々の声ぞ楽しむ。

地謡：わが腕を前に挿して悪魔を払い、引く手では寿福を

Chorus：I'm exorcising evil spirits by thrusting my arms forward, and embracing

抱き取る。かくて「千秋楽」の舞を舞い、民の心を和らげ、「萬歳楽」を舞っては万年の長寿を祝う。相生の松に楽しく風が吹き、万年の齢を寿ぐようである。(終曲)

bliss by pulling my arms back. Thus, I dance to the music of "Senshuuraku", which means "easing people's mind." Then, I dance with the music of "Manzairaku", which means "celebrating the longevity of ten thousand years." The wind is blowing and sounding merrily through the Aioi pine trees, the wind is blowing and sounding merrily through the Aioi pine trees, which has lived for ten thousand years. (The end)

中啓神扇表
Kami fan (used for the first: deity) for Noh pray -the front-

中啓神扇裏
Same as on the left -the back-

清　経
Kiyotsune

能：二番目物
Category: The Second

P. 67　さては佛神三寶も
Now that even the gods and the Buddha seemed to have...

目 次

Contents

左近衛中将清経が命を落とした。平家一門都落ちの後、柳が浦の沖で入水したのである。

清経の家臣、淡津三郎は遺髪を携えて、密かに清経の妻の下に届けに戻る。

夫の死に彼女は深く悲しみ、再会の約束を破られたことを嘆く。

夫の死を悼み悶々と夜を過ごすうちに、彼女は遺髪を宇佐八幡宮に返納してしまう。かつて一門が参篭した宮である。

彼女の夢に清経の亡霊が現れ、彼女への恋心を告げる。彼女の思いは逢瀬の喜びと破約への憤りに揺れ動く。

清経は遺髪を送り返したことについて彼女に怒りをぶつけるが、遂にはともに嘆きの涙にむせぶ。やがて清経は自死に至る経緯を打ち明け、彼女の理解を得ようとする。一門が八幡大菩薩にも見捨てられ、敵に九州をも追われたことを述べ、「あたかも追い立てられるように、この世に生き延びるよりはあの世の救いに縋りたいと、仏陀の名号を唱え、身を投げたのだった」と語る。

彼女は尚も納得しないが、清経はこれを遮り、この決断によって無常の世を逃れた喜びを訴え、「修羅道の苦しみ」から救われたのだと言う。(修羅道とは六道の一つで生前、闘争を事とした者が落ちる世界の謂いである)

中啓修羅扇

Shura fan（used for the second）for Noh play

Outline

Kiyotsune, the Sakon-ye no chūjō (Captain of the Inner Palace Guard), is dead. After leaving the capital with his clan the Taira's, Kiyotsune drowns himself on the shore of the Yanagigaura.

His retainer, Awazuno saburo, sneaks back into Kyoto to bring his wife the hair of her departed.

The death of her husband pains her deeply. She rues him breaking his promise to be with her again.

Having spent the night in agony, mourning her husband's death, she sends his hair to Usa shrine, a place where his clan prayed.

The ghost of Kiyotsune appears in her dream. He professes his love for her. His wife is torn with feelings of happiness and indignation. Kiyotsune retorts with anger at her sending his hair to the shrine.

In the end, they sob in grief together. Kiyotsune then shares what led to his death, in the hopes she will understand. He tells her the God of Arms forsook his clan, forcing them to flee from Kyushu. "It was as if he compelled me to give up living in despair in this world, and find grace in the next. Intoning the name of Buddha, I threw myself into the water."

Kiyotsune's wife cannot accept this, but he presses on, insisting that his decision has brought him joy, an escape from the uncertainty of life. He has been saved from "The agony of the Shurado". (one of six realms which those who struggle throughout their life must go to)

注 記	
作 者	世阿弥
資 材	一部は平家物語巻八に依拠するが、大半は創作されている
場 面	平家が都落ちした後の京都の清経の妻の邸。季節は晩秋、初冬 平家一門の居所。筑前の国山鹿城、豊前の国柳が浦、宇佐八幡宮、再び柳が浦、柳が浦の沖と転々とする（全て九州）

登場人物		
名 前	役 柄	能 面
清経の亡霊	シテ	中将又は今若
清経の妻	ツレ	小面
淡津三郎	ワキ	無し

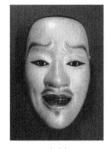

中将
Chūjō

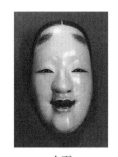

小面
Ko'omote

Notes	
Creator	Zeami
Materials	Partially based on "Tale of Heike" vol.8, but mostly dramatized.
Scenes	The mansion of Kiyotsune's wife in Kyoto from where "the Taira Clan" has already left. It's between late fall and early winter. The Taira Clan's whereabouts change from "Yamaga castle in Chikuzen Province","Yanagigaura in Buzen Province", to "Usa Shrine" "Yanagigaura" again, and to "offshore Yanagigaura" in the story. (all in Kyushu)

Characters		
Names	**Role**	**Mask**
The ghost of Kiyotsune	Shi-te (main character)	Chūjō or Imawaka
Kiyotune's wife	Tsure (minor character)	Ko'omote
Awazuno Saburo	Waki (supporting role ; foil)	No mask

それに先立ちツレ清経の妻が幕から出て、橋掛りを通り、舞台右手前のワキ座（常時ワキの座る所）に座っている。「次第」と呼ぶ登場楽（囃子）とともにワキが登場する。塗り笠を被り人目を避けた旅姿で、首に遺髪を掛けている。常座（常時シテが立つ所）に立ち、奏者（囃子方）に向き「次第」の謡を謡う。

SCENE 1 : Waki Awazuno Saburo appears, and is travelling to the capital Kyoto. Before that, Tsure Kiyotsune's wife, comes from behind the curtain and having passed through the corridor, and sitting on the "Wakiza" (usual sitting position of Waki), front stage right. With a musical accompaniment (Hayashi) called "Shidai", Waki appears, covertly outfitted with a lacquered conical hat, hanging the hair of the deceased on his neck, sings the song "Shidai" facing the musicians (Hayashikata), and is standing on the "Johza". (usual standing position of Shi-te.)

［次第］
ワキ／⌒八重の汐路の浦の波、八重の汐路の浦波、九重にいざや帰らん。

［次第の謡］
淡津三郎：遥かな八重の波路を乗り越え、遥かな八重の波路を乗り越え、無事に九重の都に帰りつこう。

[Shidai song]
Awazuno Saburo：Floating over far away eight fold waves on the sea, Floating over far away eight fold waves on the sea, I'm with little trouble coming back to the nine fold capital.

［名ノリ］
ワキ／⌒これは左中将清経の御内に仕へ申す、淡津の三郎と申す者にて候、さても頼み奉り候清経は、過ぎにし筑紫の戦に討ち負け給ひ、都へはとても帰らぬ道芝の、雑兵の手にかゝらんよりはと思し召しけるか、豊前の国柳が浦の沖にして、更け行く月の夜船より身を投げ空しくなり給ひて候、また船中を見奉れば、御形見に鬢の髪を残し置かれて候間、かひなき命助かり、御形見を持ち只今都へ上り候。

[名ノリ]

同人：私は左中将清経殿に家臣としてお仕えしている淡津の三郎です。我が主君清経殿は過日の九州での戦に打ち負け、とても都へ帰ること叶わず、豊前の国柳が浦の沖合で、月の夜更け舟より身を投げてしまわれた。此処彼処の戦場をさ迷い、名もない雑兵の手にかかって死ぬよりはと自死を選ばれたものと拝察します。さて船中を検めましたところ形見の御髪を残しておられました。この身は何とか生き延びて、ただいま御形見を持ち都に赴くところであります。

[Self introduction]

The Same：My name is Awazuno Saburo. I've been serving Sir Sachūjō Kiyotsune as his retainer. My master Kiyotsune was defeated at the battle which took place in Kyushu not long ago. He couldn't even come back to the capital, and threw himself off the ship offshore "Yanagigaura" in the Buzen province, in the middle of the night under the moonlight. I imagine he prefered to kill himself than be killed by common soldiers while wandering into various battles. Then I looked in the ship, and I found the hair of the deceased left as a memento. I've managed to stay alive, and now I'm going to go to the capital with the memento.

[道行]

ワキ／この程は、鄙（ヒナ）の住居（スマイ）に馴（ナ）れ馴れて、鄙の住居に馴れ馴れて、たまたま帰る古里（フルサト）の、昔の春に引（エ）きかへて。今は物憂（モノウ）き秋暮れて、はや時雨（シグレ）降（フ）る旅衣、萎（シヲ）るゝ袖の身の果（ハテ）を、忍（シノ）び忍びに上（ノボ）りけり、忍び忍びに上りけり。

[道行の謡]

同人：このところ長く田舎住まいを過ごしました。このところ長く田舎住まいを過ごしました。ただいまは図らずも都に戻り、往時の華やぎとは打って変わった様に驚くばかり。時は晩秋、折しもの時雨に旅の衣の袖を濡らし、かく

[Traveling song]

The same：I've led a rural lives for a long time. I've led a rural lives for a long time. Just now, I happened to come back to the capital, which looked quite different from the prosperity of old days. It was late fall and then it was drizzling, soaking the sleeves of my clothes which were worn while travelling. Thus, I've come to the capital in obscurity.

て身を潜めて都に着きました。ひっそりと上京いたしました。ひっそりと上京いたしました。

I've snuck into the capital. I've snuck into the capital.

ワキ╱急ぎ候程に、これははや都に着きて候。

淡津三郎：急ぎましたので早や都に到着しました。

Awazuno Saburo：Because I made haste, I've arrived at the capital early.

シーン2：淡津三郎と清経の妻の対話
三郎は笠を取り案内を乞う。やがてワキ座に座っているツレの許しを得て舞台に入り、中央に座り清経の死を告げる。

Scene 2 : Dialogues between "Awazuno Saburo" and Kiyotsune's wife.
Saburo is at the door, taking off his hat. After that, he enters the stage and sits at the center of it with the permission from Kiyotsune's wife who sits at Wakiza. Then he reports to her about Kiyotsune's death.

ワキ╱いかに案内申し候、筑紫より淡津の三郎が参りて候それそれ御申し候へ。

淡津三郎：申しお取次ぎを願います。九州より淡津三郎が参ったとお取次ぎください。

Awazuno Saburo：I'm sorry for bothering you, but I'd like you to tell the lady of the house I've come from Kyushu.

ツレ╱なに淡津の三郎と申すか、人までもなし此方へ来り候へ、さて只今は何の為の御使にてあるぞ。

清経の妻：なに淡津三郎か？取り次ぐまでもない、こちら

Kiyotsune's wife：Why, is this Awazuno Saburo? You don't need to bother to announce

54

にお入りなさい。この度は一
体何のお使いか？

your visit. Please come in. What message do
you have for me this time?

ワキ／さん候面目もなき御使に参りて候。

淡津三郎：はい、面目もない
お使いで参りました。申すも
憚られる次第です。

Awazuno Saburo：Well, I have a message
so pitiful. I feel really sorry telling you.

ツレ／面目もなき御使とは、もし御遁世にてあるか。

清経の妻：申すも憚られる次
第とは？　もしや清経殿はご
出家でもなさったか？

Kiyotsune's Wife：You feel really sorry
telling me? Could lord Kiyotsune have become
a reclusive priest?

ワキ／いや御遁世にても御座いなく候。

淡津三郎：いや、左様なこと
ではございません。

Awazuno Saburo：No, he didn't.

ツレ／過ぎにし筑紫の戦にも御恙なきとこそ聞きつるに、

清経の妻：過日の九州の戦で
もご無事であったとお聞きし
たが……

Kiyotsune's Wife：I've heard he was all
right even on the battle field in Kyushu these
days.

ワキ／さん候過ぎにし筑紫の戦にも御恙御座なく候ひしが、清経心に思し召す
やうは、都へはとても帰らぬ道芝の、雑兵の手にか、らんよりはと思し召され
けるか、豊前の国柳が浦の沖にして、更け行く月の夜船より身を投げ空しくな
り給ひて候。

淡津三郎：左様でございま

Awazuno Saburo：That is correct. He was

す。過日の九州の戦でもご無事でございました。私が推量いたしますに、都に帰還は叶わず、此処彼処の戦場をさ迷い名もない雑兵の手にかかって死ぬよりはと思われたのでしょう。豊前の国柳が浦の沖合で、月の夜更け舟より身を投げ、自死致されました。

all right even on the battle field in Kyushu these past days. But I imagine he may have thought that he was unable to come back to the capital, and that he preferred to kill himself than to be killed by common soldiers while wandering on various battle fields. He threw himself off the ship offshore from "Yanagigaura" in "Buzen Province", in the middle of the night under the moonlight, and drowned to death.

ツレ／〳なに身を投げ空しくなり給ひたるとや、

清経の妻：なに、身を投げ空しくなられたと？

Kiyotsune's wife：What! He drowned to death?

ツレ／〳怨めしやせめては討たれもしは又、病の床の露とも消えなば、力なしとも思ふべきに、我と身を投げ給ふ事、偽りなりつる約言かな、げに怨みてもそのかひの、なき世となるこそ悲しけれ。

同人：口惜しや、身を投げ空しくなられたとは。もしや討ち死にや病によって亡くなられたというのなら諦めもつこうというものを。必ず帰るとのお約束は嘘だったのですね。お恨み申します。ただ、お恨みしても、お亡くなりになった上は詮無いこと。ああ、なんと悲しい。

The same：How regretful that he threw himself into the water. If he was killed in a battle or died of disease, I might be able to convince myself. You lied to me. You promised to come back to me. I resent you, but it's useless to resent you after you died. Oh, what a sorrow.

[下歌]
地／何事も、はかなかりける世の中の。

[下歌の謡]
地謡：何事も不定のこの世で
は、夫婦の約束もはかないの
か？

[Sing downtone]
Chorus：Even a promise between spouses is
uncertain in this transient world, isn't it?

[上歌]
地／この程は、人目を裹む我が宿の、人目を裹む我が宿の、垣ほの薄吹く風の、
声をも立てず忍び音に、泣くのみなりし身なれども。今は誰をか憚りの、有明月
の夜たゞとも、何か忍ばん郭公、名をも隠さで泣く音かな、名をも隠さで泣く音
かな。

[上歌の謡]
同：この程は人目を忍んで
ひっそりと暮らしてきた。な
ので泣くにも只、垣根の薄を
吹く風のように、声も立てず
に涙を流していた。今は憚る
ことはない。何を忍び音にす
すり泣くことがあろうか？
夜通し鳴くという郭公のよう
に名を隠すこともなく泣き明
かそう。

[Sing uptone]
The same：Recently I had been spending
my days quietly in my house.
I was spending my days quietly in my house
where I was just shedding tears silently, like
the winds blowing through the hedge of silver
grasses.
Now I don't need to hold back. Why should I
be sobbing silently? I'm wailing like a little
cuckoo that's supposed to wail through the
night, exposing herself.

シーン3：清経の妻は夢中に清経の亡霊を待つ。

淡津三郎は彼女のお守りのために残された、亡き清経の遺髪を渡し、彼女はそれをじっと眺めて嘆く。

地謡の謡の中に清経の亡霊が登場し、入れ替わって淡津三郎は目立たぬように切戸から退場する。

Scene3 : Kiyotsune's wife is expecting Kiyotsune's Ghost to appear in her dream. Awazuno Saburo gives her the memento, the deceased Kiyotsune's hair which is left to her as a charm, while Kiyotsune's wife stares at it in grief. While the chorus is being sung, Kiyotsune's Ghost is appearing, in the place of Awazuno Saburo who is quietly disappearing towards the exit.

ワキ／また船中を見奉れば、御形見に鬢の髪を残し置かれて候、これを御覧じて御心を慰められ候へ。

淡津三郎：さて船中を検めましたところ、形見の御髪を残しておられました。どうかこれをご覧になって心をお慰めください。	Awazuno Saburo：Then I looked in the ship, and I found the hair of the deceased left as a memento. Please console yourself by looking into it.

ツレ／これは中将殿の黒髪かや、見れば目も昏れ心消え、なほも思ひの増るぞや、見る度に心づくしの髪なれば、うさにぞ返す本の社にと。

清経の妻：ああ。これは中将殿の御髪か。見るほどに悲しみがいや増し、気が遠くなり動転しそうです。彼の君の心づくしの形見なので、見るたびに悲しみが深まります。これを彼の君のまします宇佐八幡の宮に送ろうと思います。	Kiyotsune's wife：Oh, this is the hair of my Lord Chūjō! I feel faint and almost overwhelmed by looking at it, because my sorrow is deepening more and more. Because this is his heartful memento, the more times I look into it, the more my sorrow deepens. I'll send the hair to Usa Shrine in Tsukushi, where the Lord should be.

[下歌]
地ノ／手向け返して夜もすがら、涙と共に思ひ寝の、夢になりとも見え給へと、寝られぬに傾くる、枕や恋を知らすらん、枕や恋を知らすらん。

[下歌の謡]

地謡：遺髪を宇佐八幡宮に送り返し、彼女は夜もすがら夫を思い涙にくれながら眠りにつく。夢なりとも夫に相まみえることを願い、寝られぬままに夢を得んと枕をまさぐる。この枕は私の思いを夫に届けてくれるのだろうか？この枕は私の思いを夫に届けてくれるのだろうか？

[Sing downtone]

Chorus：After having sent the hair of the deceased to Usa Shrine, she goes to bed trying to fall asleep, while missing her husband and shedding tears through the night. She yearns to see her husband again at least in her dreams, but she can't fall asleep and shifts her pillow to have a dream. Just the pillow could lead him to see my yearning? Just the pillow could lead him to see my yearning?

シーン4：清経の登場

先の地謡の中に清経（亡霊）が現れ、橋掛かりを通り、常座に立つ。「恋の音取」の小書の折は、シテ登場の間に断続的に笛が独奏され、次のサシの謡を省略、＊印の箇所から演奏される。

Scene4 : Kiyotsune's appearance.

During the chorus before, Kiyotsune (his ghost) is appearing passing through the corridor and stands on the Johza. In the case of a special production "Koino Netori", intermittently played flute solo, leads him to appear, and the next phrase of recitativo is omitted, Kiyotsune's song starts from the part marked ＊.

[サシ]
シテノ／聖人に夢なし、誰あつて現と見る、眼裏に塵あつて三界窄く、心頭無事にして一床寛し、げにや憂しと見し世も夢、つらしと思ふも幻の、何れ跡ある雲水の、行くも帰るも閻浮の故郷に、辿る心のはかなさよ。

[サシの謡]

清経：聖人は徒な夢を見ない
という。凡人とても夢見る者
はそれが夢であって現のもの
でないことを知っている筈
だ。曰く、眼に塵があれば盲
となるがごとく、心に迷いあ
れば宇宙ですら窮屈だと。こ
のように考えると、この世の
どれほど苦しい体験も、移し
世の夢と思って耐えることが
でき、また多くのつらい出来
事も実際には幻だったと思う
ことができる。すべては行く
雲、流れる水の如く朧気で捉
えどころなく儚いものだ。我
が業因の故に移し世にあるも
のと知りながら、なお愚かに
も我が来し現世に心を惹かれ
ることよ。

[Sashi song]

Kiyotsune：It's said that holy saints don't
have ordinary dreams. Even dreamers who
are not holy saints should know that a dream
is just a dream, never real. As they say
people may feel like even the cosmos is
confining, if they hold worries in their heart,
as one who suffers from dust in one's eyes
gets blind. If we ponder this, the hardest
experiences in this real world will feel
endurable, like in transient dreams, and many
pitiful events actually seem to be an illusion.
Everything is as transient as clouds or
running water are vague and elusive. I realize
I live in this transient world because of my
karma. Even so, I'm foolishly attracted to the
real world where I come from.

シーン5：清経とその妻の対話

二人は言葉を交わし怨みを述べ合う。

Scene5 : Dialogue between Kiyotsune and his wife.

They are talking to each other reproachfully.

＊
シテ／假寝（ウタタネ）に、恋しき人を見てしより、夢てふものは、たのみ初（ソ）めてき。

*

清経：「うたたねに恋しい人にまみえたので、儚い夢というものを頼みにし始めた」と古歌にあるように、私もここに現れたのだ。

*

Kiyotsune：Someone said in an old poem. "I'm starting to believe in a transient dream, since I happen to meet my sweetheart in a slumber". I'm feeling like this.

シテノいかに古人（イニシエビト）、清経こそ参りて候へ（エ）。

清経：ああ愛しい其方よ。清経が来ましたよ。

Kiyotsune：My dear, I'm here!

ツレノ不思議やな睡（マドロ）む枕に見え給ふ（オ）は、げに清経にてましませども、正しく身を投げたまへ（エ）るが、夢ならで如何（イカガ）見ゆべきぞ、よし夢なりとも御姿を、見みえ給ふ（オ）ぞありがたき、さりながら命（イノチ）を待たで我と身を、捨てさせ給ふ御事（オオン）は、偽（イツワ）りなりける約言（カネコト）なれば、たゞ怨（ウラ）めしう候。

清経の妻：まどろむうちにお見えになったのはなんと不思議なこと。本当に清経殿なのですね。でもあなた様は身投げなさったはずなので、夢でしかお会いできないのですね。たとえ夢の中であっても姿をお見せくださって本当に嬉しい。でも、生きて相まみえるお約束を自死などなさって裏切られたこと、本当にお怨み申し上げます。

His wife：What a wonder you appear while I slumber! You are surely lord Kiyotsune, but I know I can see you just in my dreams because you must have drowned yourself I'm thankful that you appear in front of me even in my dreams.
Although I'm also really resentful because you betrayed your promise to meet me alive again, by killing yourself.

シテノさやう（ヨウ）に人をも怨（ウラ）み給はば、我も怨みは有明（アリアケ）の、見よとて贈りし形見をば、何（ナニ）しに返らせ給ふ（オ）らん。

清経　61

清経：其方が私を怨むという ならば、私にも其方に怨みが あります。傍に置いてほしい と思って送った形見の品をど うして送り返しなどしたので すか？

Kiyotsune：If you are reproaching me, I'd reproach you for something too.
Why did you send back the memento which I sent for you to put on?

ツレ／いやとよ形見を返すとは、思ひあまりし言(コト)の葉(ハ)の、見る度(タビ)に心づくしの髪(カミ)なれば、

清経の妻：悪気はなかったの ですが、思い余ってのこと だったのです。その時和歌に 詠んだのは「見るたびに悲し みの弥増す形見だから……

His wife：I didn't mean to do it, but I did so because I was really upset . The poem which I intoned then, said "because the more times I look into it, the more my sorrow deepens"

シテ／うさにぞ返す本(モト)の社(ヤシロ)にと、さしも贈(オク)りし黒髪(クロカミ)を、飽(ア)かずは留(ト)むべき形見ぞかし、

清経：元の宇佐八幡宮に返し ます」と。其方は言ったが、 私としては心づくしの形見な のだから、側近くに置いてお いて欲しかった。

Kiyotsune："I'll return the hair to Usa Shrine" This is what you said, despite my sending you my heartfelt memento. I wanted you to put it on.

ツレ／疎かと心得(エ)給へるや、慰(ナグサ)めとての形見なれども、見れば思ひの乱れ髪。

清経の妻：それは思い違いを なさっています。心を慰めて くれようという形見なので しょうが、逆に一層心が乱れ るのです。

His wife：You misunderstand. Although the memento is supposed to console me, it's more upsetting for me.

シテ／別きて贈りしかひもなく、形見を返すは此方の怨み。

清経：わざわざ送った形見を送り返された此方の怨み。	Kiyotsune：Well, I'd reproach you because you sent back the memento despite my sending you it.

ツレ／我は捨てにし命の怨み。

清経の妻：こちらとしては命をお捨てになった怨み。	His wife：As for me, I'd reproach you because you killed yourself.

シテ／互に啣ち、

清経：互いに怨みをぶつけ合い。	Kiyotsune：We are reproaching each other.

ツレ／啣たるゝ、

清経の妻：互いの身をかこち合い。	His wife：We repine at each other's fate.

シテ／形見ぞつらき、

清経：この形見の所為で……	Kiyotsune：Because of the memento.

ツレ／黒髪の、

清経の妻：この辛い形見の黒髪よ。	His wife：What a sorrow to see this memento of your hair.

地／＼怨みをさへに言ひ添へて、怨みをさへに言ひ添へて、くねる涙の手枕を、ならべて二人が逢ふ夜なれど、怨むれば独寝の、ふしぶしなるぞ悲しき。げにや形見こそ、なかなか憂けれこれなくは、忘るゝ事もありなんと、思ふも濡らす袂かな、思ふも濡らす袂かな。

[上歌の謡]

地謡：二人は繰り返し怨みをぶつけ合い。二人は繰り返し怨みをぶつけ合い。拗ねて泣く臥所の上で、逢瀬が永く絶えた後だというのに、背を向けているのは悲しい。まこと残念なことだ。形見の所為で慰めどころかかえって悲しみが増し、もしこれがなければ忘れることもできたのにと、二人は袖を濡らすのだった。二人は袖を濡らすのだった。

[Sing uptone]

Chorus：They are reproaching each other over and over again. They are reproaching each other over and over again. Shedding tears sulkily on the bed, they wouldn't share a bed because of their reproaching, even though they are meeting after long separation. It's really a shame. The memento gives them sorrow instead of console. Wondering if they could forget their sorrow if there was no memento, they are shedding tears. They are shedding tears

（枠内）

シーン6：清経の物語

清経は舞台中央で床几に掛かり、自死を決意するに至った経緯を語る。彼は妻に九州各地での転戦の様や宇佐八幡宮参籠のことを話すが、彼女は尚も怨みを述べる。然し清経は言葉を続け、一門が八幡大菩薩にも見放されて九州を撤退せざるをえなかったこと、彼自身も自死を選ばざるを得なかったことを語る。彼は語りつつ話に沿って戦の身振りを交えた所作を演ずる。

Scene6：Kiyotsune tells his story.

He sits on the stool at the center of the stage to tell his story about how he ended up deciding to kill himself. He tells his wife about his wanderings on various battle fields in Kyushu and visiting Usa shrine. But she still reproachs him. Then Kiyotsune persists in telling her that his legion couldn't help but withdraw from Kyushu without the protection of Hachiman Daibosatsu-Great God of Arms, and he couldn't help killing himself. He narrates his story and mimics the battles in sync with the story.

シテ／⌒ 古 (イニシエ) の事ども語つて聞かせ申し候べし、今は怨 (ウラ) みを御晴 (オンハ) れ候 (エ) へ。

清経：私が体験してきたことを話すので、どうか怨みを忘れてください。

Kiyotsune：I'll tell you how I've been, so please end your reproach of me.

［サシ］
シテ／⌒ さても九州山鹿 (キウシウヤマガ) の城 (ジョオ) へ (エ) も、敵 (カタキ) 寄せ来 (キタ) ると聞きし程に、取るものも取りあへず夜 (ヨ) もすがら、高瀬舟 (タカセブネ) に取り乗つて、豊前 (ブゼン) の国柳 (ヤナギ) と云 (イ) ふ (ウ) 所に着く、

［サシの謡］
清経：敵が山鹿の城に押し寄せてくると聞き、我等は急ぎ夜陰に乗じて船で遁れ出て、豊前の国柳というところに着いた。

[Sashi song]
Kiyotsune：We heard that our enemies would be surging toward Yamaga fortress, so we had to escape in a hurry sailing boats through the night, then we reached the shore named Yanagi（willows）.

地／げにや所も名を得たる、浦は並木の柳蔭、いと假初の皇居を定む、

地謡：真その名の通りに浦に
は柳の木が列をなしていた。
そこで我等は仮初のご座所を
造り定めたのだった。

Chorus：Indeed, fitting for the shore's name, there were willows lined up in a row. We then made a temporary palace to dwell in.

シテ／それより宇佐八幡に御参詣あるべしとて、

清経：その後宇佐八幡宮に参
詣すべしとの仰せがあって……

Kiyotsune：After that, the decision was made to pay a visit to the Usa shrine.

地／神馬七疋その外金銀種々の捧物、即ち奉幣の為なるべし。

地謡：七匹の神馬、金銀をは
じめ様々の御供物が八幡大菩
薩に捧げられた。

Chorus：Various offerings including seven sacred horses, gold and silver, were presented for the great Hachiman God of Arms

ツレ／かやうに申せば尚も身の、怨みに似たる事なれども、さすがに未だ君まし
ます、御代のさかひや一門の、果をも見ずして徒らに、御身一人を捨てし事、
実に由なき事ならずや。

清経の妻：尚も細やかな怨み
言を申しますが、帝のご治世
の成り行きや、平家一門の行
く末を見届けることなく、我
が身を空しくなさったとは申
し訳の立たない事だったので
は？

Kiyotsune's wife：I'd like to make minor complaints about you. Weren't you so senseless that you laid down your life in vain, instead of concerning yourself with the reign of the emperor and the fate of the Taira clan?

シテ／げにげにこれは御理さりながら、頼みなき世の証の告、語り申さん聞き給へ

清経：おっしゃるとおりかも知れない、が然し同時にその折に我等には、もはや見込みがないとのお告げがあったのだ。そのことをお話ししよう。

Kiyotsune：I understand, but at the same time there was a divine revelation that we had no hope of surviving. I'll tell you the story.

地／そもそも宇佐八幡に参籠し、様々祈誓怠らず、数の頼みをかけまくも、忝くも御戸帳の、錦の内よりあらたなる、御声を出して斯くばかり。

地謡：そもそも宇佐八幡宮に参詣し誠心誠意祈りを捧げ、様々な祈誓を行ったのだった。その後、恐れ多くもご宝殿の錦の帳の中よりあらたかな御声をあげてお告げがあり……

Chorus：Well, we paid a visit to Usa shrine, sincerely prayed and asked a god for various things. Afterwards there came a divine revelation in a holy voice through the silk curtain of the sanctuary. It said；

シテ／世の中の、うさには神もなきものを、なに祈るらん、心づくしに。

清経：（古歌を引いて）救いの手を差し伸べられる望みはないのに、宇佐の神に何を頼もうというのか？

Kiyotsune：(quoting an ancient poem)
What could they possibly ask the Usa God for, even though there isn't any hope of being rescued?

地／さりともと、思ふこゝろも虫の音も、弱り果てぬる、秋の暮かな。

地謡：さても救われることもあろうかと頼みに思っていたが、最早秋の終わりの虫の音のように心も弱り果てる悲しさよ。

Chorus：Well, we'd like to count on a chance to be rescued.
Although, how pitiful we are losing heart, as chirping of insects are in the end of fall!

シテ／さては佛神三寶も、

清経：さては早や神も仏も……

Kiyotsune：Now that even gods and the Buddha seemed to have

地／捨て果て給ふと心細くて、一門は気を失ひ力を落して、足弱車のすごすごと、還幸なし奉る、哀れなりし有様。

地謡：我らを捨て果て給うたかと一門心細く思い、絶望に打ちひしがれた。そして我らは帝のお供をして宇佐八幡宮から柳が浦の御所にすごすごと引き上げた。皆みじめな有様であった。

Chorus：Abandoned us, so we the Taira clan felt forlorn, overwhelmed by desperation. Then we drew back from Usa shrine to Yanagi palace with the emperor. We were all in a miserable state.

［クセ］

地／かゝりける処に、長門の国へも、敵向ふと聞きしかば、また船に取り乗りて、何処ともなく押し出す、心の中ぞ哀れなる、げにや世の中の、移る夢こそ真なれ、保元の春の花、寿永の秋の紅葉とて、散々になり浮かむ、一葉の舟なれや、柳が浦の秋風の、追手がほなる後の波、白鷺の群れ居る松見れば、源氏の旗を靡かす、多勢かと肝を消す。こゝに清経は、心に籠めて思ふやう、さるにても八幡の、御託宣あらたに、心魂に残ることわり、まこと正直の、頭に宿り給ふかと、たゞ一筋に思ひ取り。

［クセの謡］

地謡：そうこうするうち、敵が御所の対岸の長門の国に攻め寄せるとの知らせがあり、また船に乗り惨めな気持ちで、何処ともなく漕ぎ出した。この現世というものは真に不確かで移ろいやすいという外はないのだ。保元の春の折の

[Kuse song]

And then, while there was a report that our enemies would be surging toward Nagato province on the opposite shore of our palace, we miserably sailed away on the boats toward nowhere again. We realized that this real world couldn't help being very uncertain and transient. Our excess of luxuries, such as in the spring of the Hogen Period, had gone, and

ような一門の栄華の絶頂は過ぎ去り、我が一門は今や寿永の秋の紅葉と散り果て、水に浮く柳の葉のように船に漂っている。その柳が浦の秋風は我らを追い立てるように吹きつけ、白波までが追い立てて船尾を打つ。白鷺の群れ居る松を見ては源氏の大軍かと慄くばかり。こうして我清経は深く心に思うのだ。彼の八幡大菩薩のお告げはあらたかで真に理に適っている。神は正直の頭に宿り、驕る平家は助け給わぬのだ。ひたすらそのように思い込んだのだ。

our clan scattered like the autumn leaves in the Juei Period, while letting themselves drift on the boats like floating willow leaves. The autumn winds blew to drive us away, whitecaps chasing and beating the boats' tails. So we were all completely terrified to see the pinetrees crowded with white egrets, wondering if it was a large army from the Genji clan. Then I felt profoundly that the revelation of the great Hachiman was quite right, and reasonable, that gods would help the honest, not assist the haughty Taira clan. I was utterly obsessed with the thought.

シテ／あぢきなや、とても消ゆべき露の身を、

清経：如何ともしがたいこの身の状況で……

Kiyotsune：In this situation about which nothing could be done,

---

地／なほ置き顔に浮草の、波に誘はれ、船に漂ひて何時までか、憂き目を水鳥の、沈み果てんと思ひ切り、人には言はで岩代の、待つことありや暁の、月に嘯く気色にて、船の舳板に立ち上り、腰より横笛抜き出し、音もすみやかに吹き鳴らし、今様を謡ひ朗詠し、来し方行末をかゞみて、終には何時か徒波の、帰らぬは古、とまらぬは心づくしよ、この世とても旅ぞかし、あら思ひ残さずやと、外目にはひたふる、狂人と人や見るらん、よし人は何とも、みるめをかりの夜の空、西に傾く月を見れば、いざや我も連れんと、南無阿弥陀仏弥陀如来、迎へさせ給へと、たゞ一声を最期にて、船よりかつぱと落汐の、底の水屑と沈み行く、憂き身の果ぞ悲しき。

地謡：この悲運にあって、いつまで命を頼み浮草の如く漂い続けるのか？　すべてを終わらせようと心に決めて身を沈める機を窺っていたところ、夜明け方に一人船の舳先に立ち、有明月を眺め、誰かを待つふりをすることとなった。腰から横笛を取り出し、澄んだ音色を奏で、今様を謡い朗詠する。来し方行く末をつくづく考えて思い至った。人は必ず死するもの、過ぎ去った栄光は決して戻ることなく、憂いは終わることがないのだと。この世はもともと不確かな世を渡る旅であり、我が生涯に悔いはない。人目にはただ狂人と映るかも知れないが、なんと思われても構うことはない。西に傾く月を見て、ともにこの仮の世を逃れ、彼岸へ行きたいものだといよいよ思いが募る。南無阿弥陀仏弥陀如来お迎えくださいと最後の念仏を唱えて、船よりがばと身を投げ、海の底に沈んだのだった。なんとつらいことだ。

Chorus：why should we bear up under misfortune, while being attached to life, and drifting like floating weeds? I had decided to end all of this, and been waiting for the chance to drown myself. Then at dawn, I was standing alone on the bow, pretending to wait for someone under the waning moon. I took out a flute from my waist, played a clear tune, sang some "Imayoh" songs, and recited poems. I came to realize that every human beings had to end up with death, the past glorious days never came again, and sufferings would be never-ending. I decided there was nothing to regret in my whole life, because it was like a journey around the world of uncertainty to begin with. People might regard me as insane. I wouldn't care what they thought about me. I was just pining more and more to go to the other world in the company of the sinking moon to the west, fleeing from the transient world. After the last prayer saying "Namu Amidabutu Midanyorai", I threw myself overboard, and sunk down to the bottom of the sea. How pitiful I am.

彼女はなおも清経の入水を怨むが、清経は彼女を押しとどめて言う。不定のこの世から逃れ極楽浄土に再生できるよう往生を願うべきことを諭す。そして自らが堕ちた「修羅道」の苦しみを語るのだった。「修羅道」では、「無明（煩悩）」と「法性（不変の真理）」とが互いに入り乱れて激しく戦っている。然しながら遂に清経は「十念（十度の念仏）」のお蔭を以て成仏が叶った喜びを述べ、彼女に別れを告げる。

Scene7 : Ending

She still reproves Kiyotsune about his drowning himself, but Kiyotsune silences her, telling her that she should pray to die a peaceful death and to be reborn in paradise, fleeing from the uncertain world. Then he talks to her about his harsh experiences in the "Shurado", where he has ended up. There are "Mumyou" also called worldly passions and "Hosshou" also called everlasting truth, mixing and fighting strongly with each other in the "Shurado". At last, nevertheless, Kiyotsune finds a way to end up dying a peaceful death thanks to the "Junen", ten times prayer, and says his farewell to her.

ツレ／聞くにも心もくれはとり、憂き音に沈む涙の雨の、怨めしかりける契りかな。

清経の妻：お話を聞くにつけ心が塞がり、涙が雨のように流れます。なんと怨めしい夫婦の契りでありましたよ。

Kiyotsune's wife：I feel utterly hopeless hearing your story, and can't help bursting into a flood of tears. What a pity our promises have dissolved.

シテ／言ふならく、奈落も同じ泡沫の、あはれは誰も、変らざりけり。

清経：もはや何も言うなかれ。一度奈落に落ちたならば、この不定の世での勝者も敗者も皆同じ。成仏とあの世での再生が一番大切なのだ。

Kiyotsune：Stop saying any more. There is no difference between the winner and loser in this transient world, once they have fallen into the inferno. The most important thing is to die a peaceful death and to be reborn in paradise.

シテ／さて修羅道にをちこちの、

清経：さて、この私が「修羅道」に落ちると……

Kiyotsune：Well then, when I have fallen into the "Shurado".

地／さて修羅道にをちこちの、たづきは敵、雨は箭先、土は精鈊山は鉄城、雲の旗手を衝いて、驕慢の剣を揃へ、邪見の眼の光、愛欲貪恚痴通玄道場、無明も法性も乱る、敵、打つは波引くは潮、西海四海の因果を見せて、これまでなりや真は最期の、十念乱れぬ御法の船に、頼みしま、に疑ひもなく、げにも心は清経が、げにも心は清経が、仏果を得しこそありがたけれ。

地謡：さて、この私が「修羅道」に落ちると、そこここに立ち尽くす木々たちが皆敵となり、空からは矢が雨のように降りかかる。大地からは剣が無数に突きたち、山のような鉄壁の城が出現する。兵どもは雲の旗手をなびかせて挑むが如くに盾を並べ、剣を揃える。顔面は邪悪な心を映し、愛執、欲念、貪着、瞋恚、愚痴の人間のあらゆる煩悩心と涅槃に通じる人間の菩提心とが互いに入り乱れて戦っている。あたかも引き潮、上げ潮が打返すが如くである。このように九州や四国での戦の果てに、我が堕ちた「修羅道」での有様を見せたが、今はこれまで、お暇しよう。我は最後に「念仏」を唱

Chorus：Well then, when I have fallen into the"Shurado", all standing timbers turn into the enemy around there. There are falling arrows like rain from the sky, the swords are protruding from the ground together in large numbers, and a massive mountain like iron fortress appears. Defiantly soldiers are waving their flags, setting their shields and swords in array. Their faces are glaring with evil. There it looks like every human sin like worldly desires, outrage, dissatisfaction and human enlightenment like nirvana are fighting with each other in confusion. It is like ebb and high tides are waving back and forth. Thus, I've shown how I've fought in the "Shurado", where I've had to fall into, as a result of the battle in Kyushu and Shikoku. Now I'd like to say farewell. I've been able to board the ship toward paradise, thanks to my prayers for "nenbutsu". How thankful this "Kiyotsune" feels to finally have gotten to die a peaceful

72

えたおかげを以て、極楽往生
の船に乗ることができた。こ
の清経が遂に成仏を遂げ、あ
の世での再生を果たす、なん
と有難いことだ。(終曲)

death and to be reborn in paradise.

(The end)

P. 72 「邪見の眼の光」
Their faces are glaring with evil

半 蔀
Hajitomi

能：三番目物
Category：The Third

P. 94 序之舞の中
A Shot in Jo no Mai Dance

目　次

Contents

あらすじ

都北山紫野の雲林院に住む僧が、夏安居（一夏を通して行う座禅・瞑想の修行）の終わりの日に当たって、夏中供えた花のために立花供養を執り行った。

夕刻に一人の不思議な女性が現れ、とりわけ美しい花を手向ける。それは多くの花の中にあって、ひとり微笑むがごとくである。それは夕顔の花。

女性は、自分は五条辺りに住む者と言い、花の蔭に姿を隠す。真は、それは夕顔の君の幽霊であった。
(以上 前場)

さて僧が五条辺りを訪ねると、以前の通り、夕顔の這いまとう半蔀のかかった家があった。その中から女性の声が聞こえる。

僧は彼女のために回向を申し出で、やがて女性が半蔀を押し開き、その中から姿を現す。彼女は生前の光源氏とのラブロマンスを物語り、舞う。

明け方になると彼女は再び僧に回向を頼み、半蔀の中に姿を消す。

すべては僧の夢の中のようである。

中啓鬘扇表

Kazura fan（used for the Third）for Noh play -the front-

Outline

A priest who lives in Unrinnin temple in Murasakino, Kitayama in the capital, undertook the Rikkakuyou, a ceremony held to thank the flowers for their service throughout the summer season, on a day when the Geango — which means sitting indoors in Zen meditation throughout the summer — is about to finish.

In the evening, a mysterious woman appears and offers an extremely beautiful flower that seems to smile among many other flowers. It is a moonflower.

The woman says she lives around Gojō, and disappears behind the flowers. She is actually the apparition of the Lady Yūgao (moonflower).

(This concludes the first half)

Well then, the priest visits around Gojō, and he finds the house that has a Hajitomi (latticed shuttered window) with a moonflower, as it was before. You can hear the woman's voice there.

The priest offers to pray for her, and then the woman appears from behind the Hajitomi, which she pushes open. She tells him about her love story with Hikarugenji, when he was alive, and dances.

At dawn, she asks him to pray again, and disappears within the Hajitomi. That was the whole of the priest's dream.

中啓鬘扇裏
Same as on the left -the back-

注 記	
作 者	内藤 左衛門
資 材	源氏物語 夕顔の巻
場 面	前場：紫野 雲林院 僧房 夏安居の最終日 立花供養が執り行われている
	後場：同日の暮れ方　都五条の夕顔の方の邸

登場人物		
名 前	役 柄	能 面
里女	前シテ	若女
夕顔の亡霊	後シテ	同上
雲林院の僧	ワキ	無し
所の者 （雲林院近くに住む男）	アイ	無し

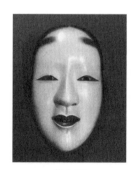

若女面

Wakaonna mask

Notes	
Creator	Saemon Naitō (reported)
Materials	Tale of Genji, vol. Yūgao
Scenes	The first half : Unrinnin temple, in Murasakino. A priest's residence where Rikkakuyou is held on the day of the end of Geango
	The second half : Later that same day, at Lady Yūgao's residence in Gojō, in the capital

Characters		
Names	**Role**	**Mask**
A woman	Shi-te in the first half	Wakaonna
The apparition of Lady Yūgao	Shi-te in the second half	The same
A priest of Unrinnin	Waki	No mask
A man living in the neighborhood of Unrinnin	Ai	No mask

シーン1：僧の登場

名宣笛の演奏につれて、雲林院の僧が幕から姿を現し、橋掛りを進み舞台に入る。僧は自らを名のり、美しい花に謝する行事を執り行う旨を述べる。やがて僧は舞台中央に進み、立花供養を執り行う。

Scene 1：A priest appears.

The priest of Unrinnin temple appears from behind the curtain, accompanied by the Nanoribue, played with the flute. He proceeds down the corridor, enters the stage, introduces himself, and makes the statement that he will undertake the ceremony thanking the flowers for serving people with their beauty. Then, he proceeds to center stage, and performs Rikkakuyou while standing there.

［名宣］

ワキ／これは紫野雲林院に住居する僧にて候、さても我一夏の間花を立て候、はや安居も過ぎ方になり、候へば、色よき花を集め、花の供養を執り行はばやと存じ候。

［名宣］

僧：私は都の紫野、雲林院に住む僧であります。
さて私はこの一夏毎日花を立ててまいりました。
今日、夏安居も終日を迎えますので、美しい花をとりそろえ、花の供養を執り行おうと思います。

[Self introduction]

The priest：I'm a priest living in Unrinnin temple, Murasakino, in the capital. Well then, I've been arranging flowers every days throughout this summer. Now, as the Geango (sitting on retreat indoors in Zen meditation for three months from April 16 to July 15) is set to finish, I'll collect beautiful flowers to undertake the ceremony of honoring the flowers for offering beauty and enjoyment for the people.

ワキ／敬って白す、立花供養の事。右非情、草木たりといへども。この花広林に、開けたり。あに心なしと言はんや、就中泥を出でし蓮、一乗妙典の題目たり、この結縁に引かれ、草木国土悉皆成仏道。

僧：（謡う）謹んで御仏に立花供養のことを申し上げます。そもそもこの花というのは心を持たぬと言われていますが、天地一面に咲き誇っています。どうして心なしと言えましょう？
なかでも泥中にあって清らに花咲く蓮は法華経の聖典のタイトルにもなっています。
この仏道との因縁に導かれ、草木国土悉皆成仏道。
たとえ心なしといわれる草木国土でも、世にあるすべてのものが成仏できますように。

The same：(singing) I'll relate in respect to you, Buddha, that I'm undertaking the Rikkakuyou. The flowers, to begin with, are blooming in the universe, even if they are supposed to be inanimate. Why do we say they aren't empathetic? Among them, lotus flowers, which bloom serene petals in the muddy pond, appear in the title of a sacred Buddhist book, Hokekyou. Led by a connection with the Buddhism, I wish "Soumokukokudo Shikkai Joubutsudou"：that everything in this world, even if they are plants or soil without feeling, may rest in peace after their death.

シーン２：里女の登場

先の僧は舞台右手前のワキ座に座っている。やがて里の女が静かな囃子の演奏（会釈〔あしらい〕）に伴われて、幕から姿を現す。橋掛りを進み、舞台に入り舞台左奥の常座に立つ。

Scene 2 : A woman appears.

The priest sits at the Wakiza, at the front of stage right. The woman then appears from behind the curtain, accompanied by very quiet music, the Ashirai, played by Hayashi. She proceeds down the corridor, enters the stage, and stands at the Johza, at the back of stage left.

シテ／手に取れば、手ぶさに穢（ケガ）る立てながら、三世（ミヨ）の仏（ホトケ）に、花たてまつる。

里女：花を手ずから摘み取るのは穢すことになります。過去、現在未来の三世のすべ

The woman：I'll offer the flowers to all the Buddhas in the three generations, past, present and future, in the state where they are

ての仏には、野にあるままに
捧げたいと思います。

growing in the field, because I don't want to
stain them by plucking them with my hands.

シーン3：僧と里女の対話

花の蔭から突如姿を現した里女に僧が語りかける。女は夕顔の花を手向けるや、自分は五条辺りに住んでいた者であると僧に告げ、やがて花の蔭に姿を消す。(中入り)

Scene 3 : Dialogue between the priest and the woman.

The priest speaks to a woman, who appears suddenly from behind the flowers. Upon offering a moonflower, the woman tells the priest that she once lived around Gojō, and then disappears behind the flowers. (intermission)

ワキ／不思議やな今までは、草花呂葉として見えつる中に、白き花のおのれひとり笑の眉を開けたるは、如何なる花を立てけるぞ。

僧：なんと不思議なことだ。
これまではどの花も同じに見えて群れ咲いていました。そ
れが今多くの花の中に、白い花が一人微笑むように見えます。何の花を供えたのですか？

The priest：What a strange thing has
happened! There have been gregariously
similar flowers so far.
A white flower now appears unlike the others,
smiling. I wonder what sort of flower you
offer.

シテ／愚かのお僧の仰せやな、黄昏時の折なるに、などかはそれと御覧ぜざる、さりながら名は人めきて賤しき垣ほに懸りたれば、知ろし召さぬは理なり、これは夕顔の花にて候。

里女：愚かなことを仰います。
黄昏時なのにそれとはおわかりにならないのでしょうか？
名は人の名のようだけれど、

The woman：You're saying a silly thing.
You should acknowledge it, because it's the
twilight hour. However, you have a good
reason not to, because the flower blooms on

みすぼらしい家の垣根に咲いているものだから、それとおわかりにならないのも、もっともなことです。
これは夕顔の花なのです。

the hedge of menial houses, although it's name sounds like that of a person.
This is a moonflower.

ワキ／げにげにさぞと夕顔（ユウガオ）の、花の主（アルジ）は如何（イカ）なる人ぞ。

僧：なるほど、これは夕顔の花でした。さてもこの花の持ち主は何方でしょうか？

The priest：I now see it's a moonflower. Well then, to whom does the flower belong?

シテ／名のらずと終（ツイ）には知（シ）ろし召さるべし、我はこの花の蔭よりまゐりたり。

里女：名のらなくても、もうおわかりでしょう。私はこの花の蔭からまいったのです。

The woman：You may acknowledge the person, without being revealed. I'm coming from behind this veil.

ワキ／さてはこの世に亡（ナ）き人の、花の供養に遇（ア）はんためか、それにつけても名のり給へ（エ）。

僧：さてはこの世に亡き人が、花の供養に立ち会おうとして姿を見せたのでしょうか。もしもそうならば、なおのこと、お名前をお聞かせください。

The priest：I now assume that you are a deceased person, appearing in order to be honored with your consecration.
If that's the case, I wish even more to know who you are.

シテ／名はありながら亡（ナ）き跡（アト）に、なりし昔の物語。

里女：確かに名はあるのですが、既に亡き身でもあり、過

The woman：Although I do have my own name, I'm a deceased person, and that' a

ぎ去った昔の出来事ですから。 | bygone story.

ワキ／何某[ナニガシ]の院にも、

僧：過ぎ去った物語と言えば、さる邸にまつわるお話が……。 | The priest：As for the bygone story, I've heard a story taking place in a certain residence.

シテ／常はさむらふ真[ロ　オ　マコト]には、

里女：実はその邸にいつもおりまして……。 | The woman：In fact, I've often been there.

[上歌]
地／五條[ゴ ジョオアタリ]辺と夕顔[イウガオ]の、五條辺と夕顔の、空目[ソラ メ]せし間[マ]に夢となり、面影[オモカゲ]ばかり亡[ナ]き跡[アト]の、立花[タチバナ]の蔭に隠[カク]れけり、立花の蔭に隠れけり。（中入）

[上歌の謡]
地謡：五条辺りに住み居りますというや、女は僧が一瞬よそ見する間に花の蔭に姿を消し、後にはその面影ばかりが残った。まるで夢のようであった。

[Sing uptone]
Chorus：After saying that she lives around Gojō, she vanishes behind the flowers in a blink of the priest's eye, leaving only her afterimages there.
It seems like a dream.

シーン4：僧と所の者（雲林院辺りに住む男）の対話

これは何事かと訝った僧は、花の供養に訪れた男（間狂言）に事の次第を尋ね、光源氏と夕顔の出会いとその物語を聞かされる。(この対話そのものはここに掲載していない)

Scene 4 : Dialogue between the priest and a man who lives in the neighborhood of Unrinnin. Upon wondering what has just happened, the priest hears the story about the affair between Hikarugenji and Yūgao, from the man (Ai) who has arrived to participate in the flower ceremony. (The dialogue itself isn't written here)

シーン5：五条辺りを訪れる僧

僧が五条辺りを訪れると、そこには夕顔の邸があり、往時のままに草が生い茂っている。間狂言（所の者）が退場すると、後見が舞台左奥の常座に半蔀の作り物を出し置く。僧は作り物の前で情景を述べる謡を謡い、謡い終わって元のワキ座に座る。

Scene 5 : The priest visits Gojō.
The priest visits Gojō, and sees the Yūgao's residence, which remains buried in overgrowth, as it was in the past. After the Ai (the man) retires, the Kohken (stage attendant) sets up the Hajitomi - shaped prop at the Johza. The priest (Waki) sings the Sashi song, standing in front of the prop, and then sits at the Wakiza.

ワキ／ありし教へに従って五条辺に来て見れば、げにも昔のいまし所、さながら宿りも夕顔の、瓢箪屡々空し、草顔淵が巷に滋し。

僧：教えられた通りに五条辺りに来てみると、昔お住まいだった頃と同じ様子です。それは漢詩に言う「孔子の十弟子中の顔淵は、瓢中に酒なく簞中に飯のない極貧にあり、その住処は草生い茂り、	The priest：According to what was said before, I visit around Gojō, and see the way she used to live in the past. It reminds me a poem from "Wakan Roueishu"：Gannen, one of the ten disciples of Confucius, used to live in destitution often without liquor to drink and food to eat, and his residence, taken over

半蔀　87

荒れ果てている」様を彷彿さ
せます。

by weeds, was desolate.

シーン6：夕顔の登場

夕顔の亡霊（後シテ）が、一声の囃子に導かれて幕から姿を現す。橋掛りを進み、半蔀の作り物の中に入る。シテの姿は見所からは確とは見えず、その謡のみが聞こえる。漢詩の一節を吟じて、茅屋の住まいを詠嘆する風情である。僧が彼女への回向を申し出ると、シテが戸を押し上げて半蔀から姿を現す。

Scene 6 : Yūgao appears.

The apparition of Yūgao (Shi-te in the second half) appears from behind the curtain, accompanied by the Issei music played by Hayashi. She proceeds down the corridor, and enters the Hajitomi-shaped prop. Her figure can't be seen ; only her singing voice can be heard. She is singing about how she feels living in her desolate mansion, while quoting phrase from Chinese poems. Upon the priest offering to pray for the repose of her soul, she shows herself from the Hajitomi, pushing it open.

［一セイ］
後シテ／藜藋（レイジョオ）深く鎖（トザ）せり、夕陽のざんせい（セキヨオ）あらたに、窓をうがつて去る、

［一セイの謡］
夕顔：藜（あかざ）の葉が茂って戸口を塞いでしまった。
夕日が山影を映し、窓から射し入っては出てゆく。

[Issei song]
Yūgao : Goosefoot weeds have grown tall and have ended up blocking the entrance. The evening sun is reflecting the mountain shape, running in and out of the windows.

地／しうたんの泉（イヅミ）の声、

地謡：山間の渓流を洗う流水の音が聞こえる。

Chorus : The sound of the welling spring water, which is flowing down into a mountain stream, can be heard.

シテ／雨原憲^{アメゲンケン}が、枢^{トボソ}を湿^{ウルオ}す。

夕顔：孔子の高弟原憲の邸の戸口に滴る雨音のように聞こえる。

Yūgao：It's like the sound of rain, which is pouring in front of the house of Genken, one of the ten disciples of Confucius.

［下歌］
地／さらでも袖を湿^{ウルオ}すは、盧山の雪のあけぼの。

［下歌の謡］
地謡：雨なくても袖を濡らす涙は、漢詩に詠まれた盧山の雪の曙の風情。

[Sing downtone]
Chorus：Tears can wet the sleeves without any rain, as quoted in "Rosan" poem.

［上歌］
地／窓東^{ソオトオ}に向ふろ^{オ ロ}うげつ^オは^タ、窓東^オに向ふろ^{オ オ}うげつ^タは、琴瑟^{キンシツ}にあたり、しうしやう^{ショ オ}の秋の山、物凄^{モノスゴ}き気色^{ケシキ}や。

［上歌の謡］
地謡：東向きの窓からは三日月が見え、琴の栫を照らし、垣根の向こうの山影が酒杯に映る。何とももの淋しい景色だ。

[Sing uptone]
The same：A crescent can be seen out of the east-facing window, and it shines upon the harp. The mountains can also be seen upon the hedge, reflecting its shape in the drinking cup. All the scenes that can be seen from Yūgao's residence is desolate.

［ロンギ］
地／げに物凄^{モノスゴ}き風の音^{オト}、簀戸^{スド}の竹垣^{タケガキ}ありし世の、夢の姿を見せ給へ^エ、菩提^{ボダイ}を深く弔^{トムラ}はん^ワ、

[ロンギの謡]

地謡（ワキの代弁）：竹垣を
吹く風の音が物凄く、寂しい。
どうかありし日のお姿を夢に
もお見せください。

[Rongi song]

The same (on behalf of the priest)：The
wind through the bamboo fence is blowing
bleakly. I'd like to see your live figure in my
dream. I will sincerely pray for the repose of
your soul.

シテ／山の端の、心も知らで行く月は、上の空にて絶えし跡の、また何時か逢ふ
べき、

夕顔：かつて和歌にも詠みま
した。山の端（光源氏）の真
意も知らずに、誘われゆく月
（夕顔）は空の果てに消えゆ
くことでしょう。
このように早や亡き身とな
り、またいつ彼の人にお逢い
できるのでしょう？

Yūgao：I once composed Waka poetry：the
moon (Yūgao), which is going to be induced
without knowing the true thought of the
mountain edge (Genji), will vanish into the
sky.
Like the poetry says, I have died all too soon,
and then I hope to see this person again.

地／山賤の、垣ほ荒るともをりをりは、

地謡：また、このようにも詠
まれました。茅屋の垣根は荒
れ果てても（お心は私を離れ
ても）時にはお訪ねください。

Chorus：Didn't you compose the poem：
despite my desolate residence's hedge
becoming bleak (losing your interest in me),
will you still sometimes come to me?

シテ／あはれをかけよ撫子の、

夕顔：撫子に情けをおかけく
ださい。

Yūgao：I sure wish that he will, for the sake
of the lovely one.

地／花の姿をまみえなば、

地謡：そのように美しいお姿をお見せくださるなら……

Chorus：If you show your beautiful self…

シテ／跡弔ふべきか。

夕顔：私のために回向願えますか？

Yūgao：Will you pray for the my repose?

地／なかなかに、

地謡：もちろんです。

Chorus：I sure will.

シテ／さらばと思ひ夕顔の、

夕顔：それならばと夕顔は……

Yūgao：Yūgao has then decided her mind.

地／草の半蔀押し上げて、立ち出づる御姿、見るに涙のとどまらず。

地謡：夕顔の蔦や花の纏わる半蔀を押し上げて、姿をお見せになった。そのお姿を見るにつけ哀れを催し、涙を止めることができません。

Chorus：She is appearing from the Hajitomi, on which moonflowers are creeping in, pushing it open.
I feel pitiful seeing her figure, and the tears gush from my eyes.

夕顔（後シテ）は邸（半蔀の作り物）から姿を現し、光源氏との情事について物語る。また、地謡が物語を謡うのに合わせて、クセの舞を舞う。

Scene 7 : Yūgao tells her story.

Yūgao (Shi-te in the second half) emerges from her residence (Hajitomi-shaped prop), and tells her story about her love affair with Hikarugenji. She also acts the standard Kuse dance, while the chorus sings the story.

［クセ］

地／その頃源氏の、中将と聞えしは、この夕顔の草枕、ただ仮臥の夜もすがら、隣を聞けば三吉野や、御嶽精進の御声にて、南無当来導師、弥勒仏とぞ称へける、今も尊きお供養に、その時の思ひ出でられて、そぞろに濡るる袂かな。なほそれよりも忘れぬは、源氏この宿を、見初め給ひし夕つ方、惟光を招き寄せ、あの花折れとのたまへば、白き扇の、端いたう焦したりしに、この花を折りて参らする。

［クセの謡］

地謡：その頃、中将 光源氏殿は夕顔の邸にかりそめの妻問いの一夜を過ごされた。夜半に僧が尊い仏典を唱える声が、「南無当来導師、弥勒仏」と隣から聞こえてくる。今、貴方様から尊いお手向けの言葉を承り、その時のことが思い出されて、涙が止まらず袖を濡らしております。

それよりも忘れ難いのは、ある夕暮源氏の君は初めてこの邸のことに心をお寄せにな

[Kuse song]

Chorus：At that time, a person named Lieutenant General Genji was staying overnight at Yūgao's residence to court her. Throughout a long night, a voice of a priest, who was reciting a phrase from the holy scripture ; may Miroku buddha bring us salvation in the near future, could be heard in the neighborhood. Your precious wish for my repose reminds me of that time, making the tears flow from my eyes, and wet my sleeves. The more memorable event was that Sir Genji ordered his attendant Koremitsu to pluck the flower for him, when he became

り、供の維光殿にあの花を折
れとお命じになったことで
す。それで私はその花を手折
り、白い扇の端に深く香を焚
きしめてその上にのせ、差し
上げたのでした。

interested in the mansion for the first time in one evening. I then plucked the flower, and offered it to him, putting it on the white-colored, heavily incensed fun.

シテ／源氏つくづくと御覧じて、

夕顔：源氏の君はそれをつく
づくとご覧になって、

Yūgao：Sir Genji was looking at it in his heart.

地／うち渡す、遠方人に問ふとても、それその花と答へずは、終に知らでもある
べきに、逢ひに扇を手に触るる、契りの程の嬉しさ、折々尋ね寄るならば、定め
ぬ海士のこの宿の、主を誰と白波の、よるべの末を頼まんと、一首を詠じおはし
ます。

地謡：それで彼の君は和歌の
一句を引いてその白い花のこ
とを私にお尋ねになりました。
「ずっと遠くにおわす其方様
にお尋ねします。その白く咲
く花は何と申すのですか？」
と。それは（私は）夕顔の花
です。と私は答えました。
もしもその時私が答えなかっ
たら、このようなお仲になる
ことはなかったでしょう。
私の差し上げた扇をお取りに
なったことがきっかけで、こ
のように結ばれ、嬉しい限り
です。この後、彼の君はしば

Chorus：He then asked me what was the white flower, quoting a Waka poem that said, I would like to ask you, being so remote what that white blooming flower is.
I answered that I am the moonflower. If I didn't, he wouldn't have begun courting me.
It was my great joy that he started to court me, by chance of his taking me up on the fun I offered.
After that, he often courted me, and became intimate with me, even though I didn't reveal my real birth and lineage because it wasn't good, and ended up composing a Waka poem.

しば妻問いをなされ、由緒正
しい身分でもないと私が素性
を明かさないにも関わらず情
を深められ、このような歌を
詠まれました。

シーン8：夕顔の舞

夕顔は源氏の詠んだ歌を吟じながら、舞にかかる。

Scene 8 : Yūgao's dance.

Yūgao (Shi-te in the second half) dances, while she recites the poem that Genji composed.

地⌒祈りてこそ。

地謡（シテの代弁）：折りて
こそ。

Chorus (On behalf of Yūgao)：I'll pluck it.

[序之舞]

後シテが序之舞を舞う。長いのど
かな囃子の演奏につれて演技する
定型の舞踏である。

[Jo no Mai Dance]

(Shi-te in the second half performs Jo no Mai dance, a long tranquil standard performance, accompanied by Hayashi.)

［ワカ］
シテ⌒祈りてこそ、それかとも見めたそかれに。

［ワカの謡］
夕顔：（舞終わり）折りてこ
そ、夕暮れにとくとみれば。

[Waka song]
Yūgao：(After finishing her dance) I'll pluck it, and look at it closer in the twilight.

地／ほのぼの見えし、花の夕顔（イウガオ）、花の夕顔、花の夕顔。

| 地謡：ほのぼのと見える美しい夕顔の花、夕顔の花よ。 | Chorus：There can be dimly seen a beautiful moonflower, a beautiful moonflower. |

シーン9：結末

後シテは再度僧に回向を頼み、明け方に半蔀の作り物に入る。これらはすべて僧の夢中の出来事のようである。

Scene 9：Ending

Shi-te in the second half asks Waki to pray for her repose again, and retires into the Hajitomi-shape prop, before dawn. That's been all in the priest's dream.

シテ／終（ツイ）の宿りは、知らせ申しつ、

| 夕顔：私の終の住処は申し上げました。 | Yūgao：I've let you know my final residence. |

地／常には訪（トムラ）ひ、

| 地謡：どうかいつもお尋ね…… | Chorus：I beg a favor of you. |

シテ／おはしませと、

| 夕顔：くださいませと…… | Yūgao：Please often visit me. |

地／木綿附の鳥の音、

地謡：言う中に早や明け方の
鳥の声も聞こえ……

Chorus：While she is begging, there can be
heard the tweet of birds in the morning.

シテ／鐘もしきりに、

夕顔：明けの鐘もしきりに
……

Yūgao：It also can be heard that the
morning bell is ringing.

地／告げ渡る東雲、あさまにもなりぬべし、明けぬ前にと夕顔の宿り、明けぬ前
にと夕顔の宿りの、また半蔀の、内に入りて、そのまま夢とぞ、なりにける。

地謡：鳴渡り、東雲の刻と
なって、あからさまになりそ
うです。夜が明け切らぬ前に
と夕顔は言い、夕顔の邸半蔀
の中へと姿を消します。
まるですべては僧の夢の中の
出来事のようでした。（終曲）

Chorus：Dawn breaks in the eastern sky,
while the morning bell is ringing. It's not
discreet if I still remain here after dawn.
Yūgao says this, and disappears into the
Yūgao's residence or Hajitomi-shape prop.
That's all been in the priest's dream.

(The end)

P. 86　空目せし間に夢となり
"She vanishes behind the flowers in a blink"

半　蔀　97

俊　寛
Shunkan

能：四番目物
Category：The Fourth

P. 121　巻き返して見れども
"So I roll back the letter to scrutinize it"

目　次

Contents

あらすじ

12世紀中頃平安時代の末期、わが国では平家一門が全盛を極めていた。法勝寺の執行の俊寛僧都は丹波の少将成経ならびに平判官康頼と一味して、俊寛の鹿ケ谷山荘で、平家一門に対する謀反を企てていた。三人は謀反を咎められ、薩摩潟の南遥かな鬼界島という孤島に流された。

時あたかも、平家一門の棟梁清盛の孫娘である中宮の安産祈願のため国々に大赦が行われ、鬼界島にも赦免使が送られようとしていた。鬼界島では、かねて信仰心が篤く熊野三社への三十三度参りを志していた成経、康頼両人が、折しも参詣の島めぐりから戻ってくる。二人は島内の其処彼処を熊野めぐりと見做して参詣しているのである。

俊寛は谷の水を汲み、それを「菊の酒」と称し二人とともに酒宴を催す。その後、赦免使が到着し、流人に大赦が与えられる旨を伝える。赦免使が赦免状を読み上げるが、なんとそこには俊寛の名がない。俊寛は仰天し、絶望の淵に沈む。赦免を受ける二人には慰める言葉もない。やがて、船は俊寛一人を残して島から出てゆく。この物語は平家物語巻三にある悲劇に基づいたものである。

中啓墨絵扇

Sumie fan（used here by Shunkan）for Noh play

Outline

In the mid-twelfth century in Japan, at the end of the Heian period, The
"Taira" clan flourished. A priest named Shunkan, who was the administrator
of Hosshouji temple, was conspiring against the Taira clan with his comrades
Naritsune, the general of "Tamba" and Priest Yasuyori, Hei Hangan, at
Shunkan's Shishigatani mountain lodge. Three of them were exiled to a
deserted island called Kikaigashima, far south across the Satsuma Sea,
accused of conspiring. At that point, the mission aiming for amnesty was
about to be sent to Kikaigashima, as well as other places of exile, because
the Taira clan was going to grant criminals amnesty, hoping for easy delivery
of their master's grandchild. On the island, Naritsune and Yasuyori, both of
whom had been godly men and aiming to perform the thirty-three visits to
the three shrines of Kumano, were now just coming back home from
wandering around the island, where they found several places which served
as substitutes of Kumano shrines. There, Shunkan was coming to meet them.
Shunkan drew water from the stream, called it "wine from chrythanthemum"
and held a party with his two comrades. After that, the missionary for
amnesty arrived there and gave them the news that they would all be
granted amnesty. The master of mission recited aloud the amnesty
declaration, but alas, Shunkan's name was not included. Shunkan was
astounded and felt desperate. The others were not able to find any words
to console him. Now, the ship was departing from the island, leaving
Shunkan on the isolated shore behind. This story is based on the tragedy
from the tale of the Heike vol.3.

注 記	
作　者	不詳
資　材	部分的に平家物語巻三を引いているが、大半は独自に戯曲化されている。
場　面	前場：治承二年初秋の都。
	後場：同年九月、鬼界島の路傍、後に島の海辺。

登場人物		
名　前	役　柄	能　面
俊寛僧都	シテ	俊寛
丹波少将　成経	ツレ	無し
平判官 康頼	ツレ	無し
赦免使	ワキ	無し
船頭（赦免使の従者）	間狂言	無し

俊寛面

Shunkan mask

Notes	
Creator	Unknown
Materials	Partially based on "Tale of Heike" vol.3, but mostly dramatized.
Scenes	The first half : The capital in early fall of the 2nd year of the Jishō Era (1180)
	The second half : September of the same year On the roadside in Kikaigashima, later on the shore of the island

Characters		
Names	Role	Mask
The priest Shunkan	Shi-te (main character)	Shunkan
Naritsune ; General Tamba	Tsure (minor)	no mask
Priest Yasuyori ; Hei Hangan	Tsure (minor)	no mask
The Amnesty Officer	Waki (supporting ; foil)	no mask
Waterman (Amnesty Officer's Follower)	Ai	no mask

赦免使（ワキ）が名宣笛の演奏に導かれて、船頭（間狂言）を従えて登場する。ワキは赦免状を懐中して常座に立ち、赦免使に任ぜられた旨をのべる。船頭役の従者に船の準備のことを命じたのち、ともに退場する。

Scene 1 : Appearance of the amnesty officer.

Waki the amnesty officer appears, accompanied by a waterman (Ai), while led by the melody of a flute (Nanoribue). He stands at Johza, carrying the amnesty letter in his bosom, and relates the story of his being appointed as the leader of the mission. He orders the waterman to prepare the boat and retires from the stage along with him.

[名宣]

ワキ／これは相国（ショオコク）に仕え申す者にて候（ソオロ）、さてもこの度中宮御産（タビチウグウゴサン）の御祈りの為（ニ）に、非常の大赦行（ダイシャオコナワ）はるるにより、国々の流人赦免（ルニンシャメンナ）ある、中（ナカ）にも鬼界（キカイ）が島（シマ）の流人（ルニン）の中（ウチ）、丹波（タンバ）の少将成経（ナリツネ）、平判官（ヘイハングヮン）康頼（ヤスヨリ）二人（ニニン）赦免の御使をば、某（ソレガシ）承つて候（ソオロオ）間、只今鬼界が島へと急ぎ候。

[名宣]

赦免使：これは太政大臣清盛公にお仕えする者である。このたびは非常の事態なので、急ぎ大赦の事が行われた。清盛公の御娘御である中宮のご安産をお祈りするため、国々の流人の赦免が行われる。なかにも某は鬼界島に流された丹波の少将成経ならびに平判官入道康頼の二名の赦免使を仰せつかったのである。これより急ぎ鬼界島に参る。

[Self introduction]

The amnesty officer : I am an officer serving the Grand Minister. (Taira Kiyomori) We made a quick decision about the amnesty because it was an urgent situation. We granted amnesty to several criminals who had been exiled, hoping in return for the easy delivery and birth of the Grand Minister's grandchild. I was appointed as the leader of the amnesty mission to grant amnesty to two people : Naritsune, the general Tamba and Priest Yasuyori, Hei hangan, who were among the criminals exiled to Kikaigashima. Now I

(従者の船頭に船の準備を命
じ、従者とともに退場する）

will hurry toward Kikaigashima.
(He orders the waterman to prepare the boat
and retires from the stage with him.)

シーン2：成経、康頼の登場

二人が次第の囃子に導かれて、幕から姿を現す。橋掛りを進み、舞台に入り、舞台中央で対面するや、

次第の謡を謡い、続いて自らを名のり境遇を述べる。謡い終わると、二人は舞台中央から地謡前へ移

動する。

　注：次第の囃子は演者が橋掛りを進む間、静かに演奏される登場楽である。

Scene 2 : Naritsune and Yasuyori appear.

The two of them appear from behind the curtain guided by the sound of
Shidai music, played by Hayashi. They proceed down the corridor, enter the
stage, and face each other on the center of the stage, singing the Shidai
song and introducing themselves. Then, they left the center of the stage to
move to the front of the back chorus sitting group.

　c.f. Shidai music : tranquil music played by Hayashi members as the players
　　proceed down the corridor.

［次第］
成経、康頼／神を硫黄が島なれば、神を硫黄が島なれば、願ひも三つの山ならん。

［次第の謡　連吟］
成経、康頼（連吟）：この島
は神を祝う（硫黄）島の別名
を持っています。なので私た
ちは熊野詣でと見立てて参詣
し、このように神に願いを、
神に願いを立てているのです。

[Shidai song　singing together]
Naritsune & Yasuyori：（singing together）
This island is called Ioh, which means giving
thanks to God. We visit the esteemed shrines
of Kumano and revere the gods. Thanks to
our reverential actions, thanks to our
reverential actions, may the gods bless us,
may the gods bless us.

これは九州薩摩潟、鬼界が島の流人の中、

[サシの謡]

同両人：私達は鬼界島という
離島に流された流人でありま
す。二人の中……

[Sashi song]

The same：We have been exiled to a deserted
island called Kikaigashima. Among us,

成経／〵丹波の少将成経、

成経：私は丹波の少将成経
……

Naritsune：this is Naritsune, the general of
Tamba.

康頼／〵平判官入道康頼、

康頼：私は平判官入道康頼と
申します。

Yasuyori：and I am Priest Yasuyori, Hei
Hangan.

成経、康頼／〵二人が果てにて候なり。我等都に在りし時、熊野参詣三十三度の、歩
みを為さんと立願せしに、その半ばにも数足らで、かかる遠流の身となれば、
所願も空しくはやなりぬ、せめての事の余りにや、この島に三熊野を勧請申
し、都よりの道中の、九十九所の王子まで。

成経、康頼（連吟）：二人は
謀反の咎で流罪となりまし
た。都にいた時、私たちは熊
野三十三度詣りを成し遂げん
と発願しました。しかしなが
らこのような絶海の孤島に流
罪となり、願いは空しくなり
ました。そこで切なる願いの
あまりに、本宮、新宮、那智

Naritsune & Yasuyori：(singing together)
The two of us have been executed for the
conspiracy. When we lived in the capital, we
hoped to accomplish the 33 visits to the
Kumano shrine. However, our hopes went up
in smoke because of the exile to this remote,
deserted island. Well then, as the results of
our aspiring reverence, we are planning to
invite the gods of the three main shrines,

の三熊野の神をお迎えしよう
と……。あまつさえ九十九箇
所の王子社までも。

Hongu, Shingu and Nachi, as well as the 99 minor Ohji shrines.

[下歌]
成経、康頼／悉(コトゴト)く順礼(ジュンレイ)の、神路(シンロ)に幣(ヌサ)を捧げつつ。

[下歌の謡]
同両人：ことごとく諸社を擬え造り、順次参詣して御幣を捧げるのだ。

[Sing down tone]
The same：We come to concoct all those shrines, visit every place and make offerings to them.

[上歌]
成経、康頼／此処(ココ)とても、同じ宮居(ミヤキ)と三熊野の、同じ宮居と三熊野の、浦の浜木(ハマイ)綿一重(ウヒトエ)なる、麻衣(アサギヌ)の萎るるを、ただそのままの白衣(ハクエ)にて。真砂(マサゴ)を取りて散米(サンマイ)に。白木綿花(シライウバナ)の御祓(ミソギ)して、神(カミ)に歩(アユ)みを運(ハコ)ぶなり、神に歩みを運ぶなり。

[上歌の謡]
同両人：この孤島でも、此処
彼処を尊い御熊野と此処彼処
を尊い御熊野と見做して、この
ように尊拝しているのです。粗
末な麻衣一重だけを着ての参
拝で、浜に百重に咲き繁る浜
木綿とは対照的です。それも
海潮と我らが涙で濡れそぼっ
ています。我らはまた、浜のい
さごを散米に、浜木綿を清め
の御幣に替えて、神前に参る
のです。神前に参るのです。

[Sing up tone]
The same：Even on this deserted island, we perform these acts of reverance because we esteem the places as the sacred three shrines, as the sacred three shrines.
We wear only thin linen clothes drenched with salt water and our own tears, in contrast to the crinum here on the shore flourishing thickly. We also make an offering of seashore sand instead of holy rice, perform a purification with crinum flowers instead of the sacred Gohei wand. Thus, we visit the sacred shrines, we visit the sacred shrines.

シーン3：俊寛の登場

一声の囃子に導かれて、俊寛が幕から姿を現す。橋掛りを進み、その中程過ぎにて立ち止まり、正面向いて一セイの謡を謡う。続いてサシの謡を謡うなかに再び橋掛かりを進み、舞台に入り謡の終わりに常座に立つ。

> 注：一声の囃子は演者が橋掛かりを進む間に演奏される、静かで、ややアップテンポな登場楽である。

> 注：常座はシテがしばしばそこに立つ舞台上の特定のポジションで、舞台左奥に位置する。

Scene3 : Shunkan appears.

Shunkan appears from behind the curtain guided by the sound of Issei music, played by Hayashi. He proceeds down a corridor named Hashigakari, comes to a halt in the middle of the corridor, and sings the Issei song. Sequentially, he sings the Sashi song, and proceeds down the corridor until he steps onto the stage and stands on Johza at the end of the Sashi song.

> c.f. Issei music : tranquil but a little up-tempo music played by Hayashi members as The players proceed down the corridor.

> c.f. Johza : the specific position on the Stage where Shi-te often stands, located in the back left of the stage.

［一セイ］
シテ／後の世を、待たで鬼界が島守と、

［一セイの謡］	[Issei song]
俊寛：この世に生きながらにして、「鬼の棲む」というこの地獄のような島の住人に……	Shunkan：I have become an inhabitant of this hellish island named Kikai, which means "Demons Dwelling," while I'm still living.

地／なる身の果の冥きより、

地謡：なってしまった。そしてこの身は冥途の暗闇に入っていくようだ。	Chorus：And it seems like I am entering the darkness of the hell.

シテ／冥き途<ruby>冥<rt>クラ</rt></ruby>き<ruby>途<rt>ミチ</rt></ruby>にぞ入りにける。

俊寛：そうだ、もともと心の闇を抱えていたところに、今や真の暗闇に囲まれてしまっているのだ。

Shunkan：Yes, I used to somewhat live in a state of darkness of my mind, and now I have really found myself in the darkness.

［サシ］

シテ／<ruby>玉兎<rt>ギョクト</rt></ruby><ruby>昼眠<rt>ヒルネム</rt></ruby>る<ruby>雲母<rt>ウンボ</rt></ruby>の<ruby>地<rt>チ</rt></ruby>、<ruby>金鶏<rt>キンケイ</rt></ruby><ruby>夜宿<rt>ヨルシュク</rt></ruby>す<ruby>不萌<rt>フボオ</rt></ruby>の<ruby>枝<rt>シ</rt></ruby>、<ruby>寒蟬<rt>カンセン</rt></ruby><ruby>枯木<rt>コボク</rt></ruby>を<ruby>抱<rt>イダ</rt></ruby>きて、<ruby>鳴<rt>ナ</rt></ruby>き<ruby>尽<rt>ツク</rt></ruby>くして<ruby>頭<rt>コウベ</rt></ruby>を<ruby>回<rt>メグ</rt></ruby>らさず、俊寛が身の上に知られて候。

［サシの謡］

同人：月世界の兎は昼中、不死の世界に眠るといい、太陽の鶏は夜、枝葉のない木に留まるという。秋の蟬は古木を抱いて鳴き尽くし、身動きもしない。昼間の月、夜の太陽、秋の蟬、これらは皆、今の我が身の上を表しているようだ。

[Sashi song]

The same：The rabbit in the moon is said to sleep in the immortal world during the daytime, and the cock in the sun is said to stay in the branch of the bare trees in paradise at night. Autumn cicadas stop on the dead tree, and neither chirp nor stir. The moon by day, the sun at night and autumn cicadas, all of these reflect my states of being.

康頼は成経とともに地謡前に立ち、俊寛に話しかける。俊寛は両人に対面し、手には菊の水に見立てた水の入った桶を持っている。三人は着座し、水を酒と見做して酌み交わし、物思いに耽る。地謡が上歌の謡を謡うなか、俊寛は立ち上がって辺りを眺めやり、手に持つ舞扇で、散る木の葉を受けながら憂き身を嘆き、遂には悲しみに身を臥せる。

Scene4：Shunkan's dialogue with Naritsune and Yasuyori.
Yasuyori, standing in front of the back chorus sitting group, talks to Shunkan, together with Naritsune. Shunkan is facing the two of them, holding a pail with water which he takes dewdrops of chrysanthemum. The three of them sit and drink together with water they imagine to be liquor, lost in thoughts. While the chorus sings up-tone, Shunkan stands up, takes a look around the scene, grieves deeply about their situation, receives falling leaves with his fan, " Mai-Ohgi", and at last, he gets down on his knees with sorrow.

康頼／あれなるは俊寛にて渡り候か、これまでは何の為に御出でにて候ぞ。

康頼：これは俊寛殿。何故こちらまでお出でになりましたか？	Yasuyori：Here is Shunkan. Why do you come here?

シテ／早くも御覧じ咎めたり、道迎へのその為に酒を持ちて参りて候。

俊寛：早くも見咎められましたか。熊野参詣からのお帰りを出迎えようと、この酒を持って参りました。	Shunkan：So soon you find me. I was waiting for you to come back from your visit to the shrines, and treating you with this liquor.

康頼／そも一酒とは竹葉のこの島にあるべきかと、立ち寄り見れば、や、これは水なり。

康頼：なんとこの島に酒など
あるのかと。よく見れば、こ
れは水ではありませんか？

Yasuyori：Why does liquor exist here in this
desolate island? I look at closely. Well, it's just
water.

シテ／これは仰せにて候へども、それ酒と申す事は、もとこれ薬の水なれば、
醴酒にてなどなかるべき。

俊寛：そう仰いますが、酒は
もともと谷水から造られるも
の。これを美酒と思えば良い
のですよ。

Shunkan：You say so, but originally, liquor
is made from rill water, so we can consider
this to be pure liquor.

康頼、成経／げにげにこれは理なり、頃は長月。

康頼、成経：（連吟）なるほ
ど、そのとおり。時は正に九
月。

Yasuyori & Naritsune：We find that makes
sense. It is September now.

シテ／時は重陽、

俊寛：また、菊の節句重陽の
時でもあり……

Shunkan：It is also the festival of the
chrysanthemum "Choyo-no- Sekku."

康頼、成経／所は山路。

康頼、成経：（連吟）所は山
路です。

Yasuyori & Naritsune：Here is a mountain
pass.

シテ／谷水の、

俊寛：水は谷水……

Shunkan：Liquor from rill water.

康頼、成経、俊寛／彭祖が七百歳を経しも、心を汲み得し深谷の水。

康頼、成経、俊寛：（連吟）
仙人「彭祖」が七百歳を生き
たのも、清らかな谷水の功徳
でした。それが、仏教の聖典
「法華経」の記された菊の葉
の露から流れ出たものだと
知って飲んでいたのです。

Yasuyori & Naritsune, Shunkan (all together)：They are the benefits of rill water that hclpcd "Houso", the saint live to be 700 years old. He drank it, knowing that it came from the dewdrops of chrysanthemum leaves on which the holly Buddhist scripture "Hokekyou" was written.

［上歌］

地／飲むからに、げにも薬と菊水の、げにも薬と菊水の、心の底も白衣の、濡れて干す、山路の菊の露の間に、我も千年を経る心地する、配所はさても何時までぞ。春過ぎ夏闌けてまた、秋暮れ冬の来るをも、草木の色ぞ知らするや、あら恋しの昔や、思ひ出は何につけても。あはれ都に在りし時は、法勝寺法成寺、ただ喜見城の春の花、今は何時しか引きかへて、五衰滅色の秋なれや、落つる木の葉の盃、飲む酒は谷水の、流るるもまた涙川、水上は我なるものを、物思ふ時しもは、今こそ限りなりけれ。

［上歌の謡］

地謡：飲むうちに功徳を受け
る谷の水、功徳を受ける谷の
水。それは聖なる菊の葉に宿
る露の水だからです。山路を
行くうちに我らが袖も濡れそ
ぼちます。その袖の乾く短い
間と思ったが、実は仙人が千
年を過ごした時間だったと古
歌に言います。それにつけて
もいつまでこの流刑地で過ご
さなければならないのでしょ
うか？　春が過ぎ夏も終わり

[Sing up- tone]

Chorus：When we drink rill water, when we drink rill water, we relish its benefit, we relish its benefit. Because it comes from the dewdrops of the holy chrysanthemum leaves. While we stroll through the mountain pass, our clothes are drenched with the dewdrops of chrysanthemums. We feel the short time it takes for our clothes to dry is as long as the saint's life of a thousand years. Oh, how long we do have to be confined to the island? Spring has passed, summer is over, autumn has ended, and winter is coming. All of that,

114

秋も暮れ、冬が来ようとしています。これらは皆草木の色が変わることで知るばかりです。昔の栄華が恋しく、思い出は身を責める。ああ、我らが都にいた折には、法勝寺や法成寺といった大寺に住み、そこではかの喜見城に咲き誇るという春の花のように栄えていました。今ではそれに引き換えて、萎れ枯れ落ちる秋の葉のような身の上です。酒に見立てて木の葉の盃に受けて飲む谷水も、我らの涙が流れてできたかのようです。元はと言えば我ら自身の身から出た錆で、ただ嘆くよりほかはありません。

we just know through changing colors of leaves and grasses. We really pine for the past, when we are flourished. These memories are always poignant for us. Alas, when we lived in the capital, we so flourished, living in the great temples, including Hosshouji and Houjouji, where we were in full bloom like the spring flowers in the great Kikenjoh. We have now come to ruin instead, like the autumn leaves that are withering and falling. We drink the rill water, which we imagine to be liquor, with the cup of the leaves. Even rill water looks like it is made from our own tears. We know we have brought the ruinous situation upon ourselves, and can not help but grieve deeply.

シーン5：赦免使の到着

後見が鞆綱をつけた船の作り物を舞台近くの橋掛り（一の松）に置く。一声の囃子につれて後ワキ（赦免使）が船頭を従えて登場、両名は船中に立つ。船頭は棹を持つ。続いて赦免使は一セイの謡を謡い、その後船頭は赦免使が鬼界島に到着した旨を告げる。赦免使は船より降り、船頭は船を橋掛りの壁に立て掛けた後、狂言座（橋掛り上の舞台に近い所）に座る。

Scene5 : Arrival of the amnesty officer.

The stage attendant sets down a boat with attached a rope in the corridor at the part near the stage. Then, Waki in the second half (the amnesty officer) followed by the waterman appears, and both of them board the boat, the waterman holding a pole with his hands. After that, the amnesty officer sings an issei song and then the waterman announces the arrival of the amnesty officer at the Kikaigashima. The amnesty officer leaves the boat, and the waterman sits on Kyōgenza, a specific position in the corridor close to the stage, after standing the boat against the back wall.

［一セイ］
後ワキ／早舟（ハヤブネ）の、心に叶ふ追風（カノオオイテ）にて、舟子（フナコ）やいとど勇むらん。

［一セイの謡］
赦免使：追風に乗って、船足が速く、舟子たちも一層勇気づけられることだ。
（船頭は船が到着したことを告げ、赦免使は船を降りる）

[Issei song]
Amnesty officer：The boat has been so fast sailing with a favorite following wind, that the watermen have to feel more encouraged.
(The waterman announces the arrival of the boat and the amnesty officer leaves the boat)

シーン6：赦免使と俊寛たちとの対話

赦免使は赦免状を手に持ち、目付柱（舞台の左手前角の柱）近くに進み、赦免状を俊寛に手渡す。俊寛はそれを康頼に渡し、読み上げるように促す。

さてそこで、俊寛は自分の名前がないことに仰天し、赦免状を取り戻すが、やはり自分の名がないことを確かめ、悲嘆に暮れる。

その後も何度も読み返すが、やはり何処にもその名はない。遂に絶望のあまりに赦免状を投げ捨て、身を打ち臥せる。成経は赦免状を拾い上げ、懐中する。ドラマが進展するうち、クセの謡の終わりに赦免使と船頭は、橋掛りーの松で再び乗船する。

Scene6 : The amnesty officer's dialogue with Shunkan and his comrades.

The amnesty officer, holding the amnesty letter in his hand, comes forth near the Metsuke Pole (standing at the front corner of the stage left), and hands Shunkan the letter. Shunkan passes it to Yasuyori and lets him read aloud. Well then, Shunkan is really astounded not to hear his own name, so takes back the letter to make sure his name is not there, and ends up in deep grief. After that, Shunkan looks at the letter repeatedly, in vain. At last he abandons the letter and acts with gestures of despair. Naritsune takes the letter and places it in his bosom. As the drama unfolds, at the end of a Kuse song, the amnesty officer and waterman board the boat again at the Ichinomatsu in the corridor.

ワキ／いかにこの島に流され人^{ヒト}の御座候か、都より赦免状^{シャメンジョオ}を持ちて参りて候、急いで御拝見^{ハイケン}候へ^エ。

赦免使：申し、この島に流罪人が居られるか？　都より赦免状を持参致した。急いで拝見されたい。

Amnesty officer：I wonder if there are exiled criminals. I will say that I am coming and bringing the letter of amnesty from the capital. Please take a look at it soon.

シテ／あらありがたや候、軈て^{ヤガ}康頼御覧候へ^エ。

俊寛：これは有難いことだ。康頼殿、すぐに読み上げられよ。

Shunkan：I am so grateful. Yasuyori should read it aloud in a hurry.

康頼〽何々中宮御産の御祈りの為に、非常の大赦行はるるにより、国々の流人赦免ある。中にも鬼界が島の流人の中、丹波の少将成経、平判官入道康頼二人赦免ある処なり。

康頼：何々、太政大臣殿の御孫御安産のお祈りのために非常の大赦が行われたので、国々の流罪人が赦免になる。そのなかに、鬼界島に流された丹波の少将成経ならびに平判官入道康頼の両名が赦免されるものである。

Yasuyori：Well, it says that an amnesty urgently took place, for the purpose of hoping for the easy delivery of the Grand Minister's grandchild, so several criminals were granted release. Among them, Naritsune, the general of Tamba and Priest Yasuyori, Hei Hangan, both exiled in this Kikaigashima are to be freed now.

シテ〽何とて俊寛をば読み落とし給ふぞ。

俊寛：何故に俊寛の名を読み落とされるのだ。

Shunkan：Why on earth did you make the error of not calling my name?

康頼〽御名はあらばこそ、赦免状の面を御覧候へ。

康頼：お名前がないのです。赦免状をよくご覧ください。

Yasuyori：Your name is not here. Please take a closer look at the letter.

シテ〽さては筆者の誤りか。

俊寛：これは筆者の書き損じなのか？

Shunkan：This is the writer's mistake, isn't it?

ワキ／いや某（ソレガシ）都にて承り候も、康頼成経二人（ニニンナ）は御供申せ、俊寛一人（イチニンノ）をばこの島に残し申せとの御事にて候。

赦免使：いやいや、某が都でご命令を受けたのも、康頼、成経の二人を連れ戻せ、俊寛一人は残せとのことであった。	Amnesty officer：Not at all. I got the order at the capital, saying that I was expected to take back the two, Yasuyori and Naritsune, and leave just Shunkan on the island.

シテ／こは如何（イカ）に罪も同じ罪（ツミ）、配所も同じ配所（ハイショ）、非常も同じ大赦（タイシャ）なるに、ひとり誓（チカ）ひの網に洩（モ）れて、しづみ果てなん事は如何（イカ）に。

俊寛：これは一体なんとしたことだ。我ら三人は正に同じ罪に問われ、正にこの同じ島に流されたのだ。しかも正に同じ非常の大赦が行われた。流された我ら三人のなかで、何故我一人が残されるのか？ 神仏も我を見捨て賜うたか？	Shunkan：How on earth can this happen? The three of us have been accused of the very same crime and are remained in prison in the very same place. Then the very same amnesty took place. Among all of us who have been imprisoned, why am I the only one left here? I really wonder if even the gods have forsaken me.

［クドキ］
シテ／この程は三人一所（イッショ）に在（ア）りつるだに、さも恐ろしく凄ましき、荒磯島（アライソジマ）に唯一（タダヒト）人、離（リ）れて海士（アマ）の捨草（ステクサ）の、波の藻屑（モクズ）の寄辺（ヨルベ）もなくて、在（ア）られんものか浅ましや、嘆（ナゲ）くにかひも渚（ナギサ）の千鳥、泣くばかりなる有様かな。

［クドキ］ 同人：この島は荒磯に囲まれ、これまで三人一緒でさえも恐ろしく寂しいのに、今一人残されて如何生きてゆけるのか？ 海士の捨てた海藻が波に漂うような心もとない気	[Lamentation] The same：It's so desolate here on this island surrounded the rough shoreline that I have terribly felt lonely and helpless, even with my comrades. Now, how can I survive here just by myself? I feel I am living with so many uncertainties, as though the seaweed is

持ちだ。甲斐のないことなが
ら泣くよりほかない有様だ。

drifting along the tide. I can't help but weep bitter tears, although I know well that it is useless.

[クセ]

地／時を感じては、花も涙も濺ぎ、別れを恨みては、鳥も心を動かせり、元より
もこの島は、鬼界が島と聞くなれば、鬼ある所にて、今生よりの冥途なり、た
とひ如何なる鬼なりと、この哀れなどか知らざらん、天地を動かし、鬼神も感を
なすなるも、人のあはれなるものを、この島の鳥獣も、鳴くは我を間ふやらん。

[クセの謡]

地謡：花でさえ感動する時に
は涙を流し、別れを悲しむ時
には鳥も心を動かすものであ
る。言うまでもなくここは鬼
界島といって「鬼が棲む」よ
うな島で、実際にこの世の地
獄のようである。しかしなが
らたとえ鬼であっても、この
我の深い悲しみを感じ取らな
いことがあるだろうか。人の
悲しみというものは、時に天
地をも動かし、鬼神をも感動
させるのであるから。この島
の鳥や獣までも我を慰めてく
れているようだ。

[Kuse song]

Chorus： When they are moved, even flowers drop their tears, and when they feel the sorrow of parting, even birds are really touched in the heart. As is widely known, here is the island of Kikaigashima, which means "Demon Dwelling", and it seems like a dwelling, indeed, looking like hell on earth. However, even demons should perceive this deep sorrow of mine. For, as they say, one's deep sorrow can move heaven and earth, and even though the demons. The birds and beasts of the island also look like consoling me.

シテ／せめて思ひの余りにや、

俊寛：我は思いのあまりに確
かめようと……

Shunkan：I'm so desperate to make sure,

地ノ／前に読みたる巻物を、また引き抜き同じ跡を、繰り返し繰り返し、見れども見れども、ただ成経康頼と書きたるその名ばかりなり、もしも礼紙にやあるらんと、巻き返して見れども、僧都とも俊寛とも、書ける文字は更になし、こは夢かさても夢ならば、覚めよ覚めよと現なき、俊寛が有様を、見るこそ哀れなりけれ。

地謡：一度読んだ巻物をまた引き広げ、繰り返し見る。しかしながら何度読んでも、ただ、成経、康頼の名ばかり、我の名は見当たらない。もしかして追記にでもあるかと巻き返してみる。でも僧都とも俊寛とも書かれた文字はどこにもない。我は惑い、悪い夢を見ている心地で、夢から覚めよ、覚めよと願うばかりで……なんともはた目にも哀れな有様であった。

Chorus：that I take the rolled letter again, unroll it, and look at it repeatedly. However, there are just the name of the two, Naritsune/Yasuyori and no name of mine at all. I wonder if it is written in the appendix, so I roll back the letter to scrutinize it. Alas, I find nothing of letters like "Priest" or "Shunkan". I'm distraught, feeling like I'm in an ominous dream, and I crave getting out of it, getting out of it right now. Oh, what a pitiful situation this is!

シーン7：一行の船出

船に乗った赦免使一行は成経、康頼両名を呼び寄せる。俊寛は康頼の袂に取り付くが、赦免使が押し戻す。そこで俊寛は舫綱に取り付くが船頭が綱を断ち切る。俊寛は渚に倒れ泣き伏す。

Scene7：The party is at the sea.

The troupe of the amnesty officer on the boat calls for the two, Naritsune/Yasuyori. Shunkan clings to Yasuyori's sleeve, and the amnesty officer pushes Shunkan back. Well then, Shunkan clings to the mooring line of the boat, but it's cut off by the waterman. Shunkan ends up lying down on the shore, bitterly weeping.

ワキ／時刻移りて叶ふまじ、成経康頼二人ははや、お船に召され候へとよ。

赦免使：潮時に船出せんとて遅延はならない。成経、康頼両名は疾く乗船されよ。

Amnesty officer：We shouldn't be late, because we want to set sail at high tide. The two Naritsune/Yasuyori are better off on board.

康頼、成経／かくてあるべき事ならねば、外の嘆きを振り捨てて、二人は船に乗らんとす。

康頼、成経：我らは俊寛を振り捨てても行かざるを得ません。乗船しよう。

Yasuyori/Naritsune：We can't help but go along, shake Shunkan off, and we are going to board.

シテ／僧都も船に乗らんとて、康頼の袂に取りつけば、

俊寛：我も船に乗らんと康頼の袂に取り付く。

Shunkan：I'm going to get on board too, and I'll try to cling to Yasuyori's sleeve.

ワキ／僧都は船に叶ふまじと、さも荒けなく言ひければ、

赦免使：俊寛僧都は乗船罷りならぬと激しく言い捨て……

Amnesty officer：I'll say harshly that Priest Shunkan is never allowed to board.

シテ／うたてやな公の私と言ふ事のあれば、せめては向ひの地までなりとも、情に乗せて賜び給へ。

俊寛：なんと心ない。「公の私」ということもあるではないか？　せめて対岸の九州の地まででも、どうかお情けで乗せていってくれ。

Shunkan：What a heartless person. Isn't there something you've heard of called "Principles but with compassion?" Please at least bring me to the opposite shore of Kyushu, with your blessing.

ワキ／情も知らぬ舟子ども、櫓櫂を振り上げ打たんとす。

赦免使：無情な船頭は櫓櫂を
振り上げ、俊寛を打とうとする。

Amnesty officer：The ruthless waterman
will about to hit Shunkan with his pole.

シテ／さすが命の悲しさに、又立ち帰り出船の、纜に取りつき引き留むる。

俊寛：打たれまいと退いて、
俊寛は船の纜に取り付き引き
留めようとする。

Shunkan：To avoid being hit, Shunkan steps
back and clings to the mooring line of the
boat.

ワキ／舟人 纜 押し切つて、船を深みに押し出す。

赦免使：船頭は纜を押し切っ
て、船を深みに押し出す。

Amnesty officer：The waterman will cut it
off、and sail the boat to the water's depths.

シテ／せん方波に揺られながら、ただ手を合はせて船よなう。

俊寛：仕方なく、海中で波に
揺られながら手を合わせ、船
に向かって叫ぶ。「どうか船
に乗せてくれ」と……

Shunkan：I can't help but float in the waves,
praying with hands folded, calling for the
boat. "Please take me onto the boat!"

ワキ／船よと言へど乗せざれば。

赦免使：汝を乗せることは罷
りならぬ。

Amnesty officer：You are never allowed on
board.

シテ／力及ばず俊寛は、

俊寛：力果てて断念し……

Shunkan：I give up.

地／もとの渚にひれ伏して、松浦佐用姫も、我が身にはよも増さじと、声も惜しまず泣き居たり。

地謡：もとの渚にひれ伏して、松浦佐用姫の悲劇もかくやとばかり、激しく泣き叫ぶのだった。

Chorus：Lying down on the shore, Shunkan is crying and weeping so bitterly, as Lady Matsurasayo does in her tragedy.

船よと言へど乗せざれば

You are never allowed on board

ただ手を合わせて船よなう

praying with hands folded, calling for the boat

シーン8：結末

赦免使、成経、康頼の三人は船中に立ち、俊寛に向かってロンギの謡を謡いかける。俊寛は舞台上に下居して三人に謡い返す。このやりとりが繰り返され、やがて地謡が謡うなかに三人は船より出て橋掛りから幕中へ退場、俊寛は立ち上がり、涙とともに一行を見送る。

Scene8 : Ending

The three, the amnesty officer, Naritsune, Yasuyori, who are standing on board, sing the Rongi Song to Shunkan, who sits on the stage. Shunkan sings back to them, and this sequence is repeated. While the chorus is singing, the three retire from the stage (corridor), when Shunkan stands up, and sees them off, weeping.

赦免使、成経、康頼／傷わしの御事や、我等都に上りなば、宜きやうに申し直しつつ、軈て帰洛はあるべし、御心強く持ち給へ、

[ロンギの謡]

赦免使、成経、康頼：おいたわしいことです。我らが帰洛の暁には良いようにお執り成しいたしましょう。その結果御身のご帰洛も叶うでしょう。どうかお気を強くお待ちください。

[Rongi song]

Amnesty officer, Naritsune, Yasuyori：
It's so pitiful. When we come back to the capital, we will work on your behalf. You may return home as well. Please wait patiently.

シテ／帰洛を待てよとの、呼ばはる声も幽かなる、頼みを松蔭に、音を泣きさして聞き居たり、

俊寛：帰洛を待てとの声にかすかな望みを抱いて、我は渚の松蔭の下で耳をそばだてている。

Shunkan：I'm pricking up my ears, under the pine tree on the shore, waiting with a glimmer of hope that I will be able to return home.

赦免使、成経、康頼／聞くや如何にと夕波の、皆声々に俊寛を、

赦免使、成経、康頼：我らは声々に我らの声を聴いているかと呼びかけ……

Amnesty officer, Naritsune, Yasuyori：
We are calling respectively if you are hearing.

シテ／申し直さば程もなく、

俊寛：取りなしてもらえれば、すぐにでも……

Shunkan：If you say well to intercede with me, I may soon.

赦免使、成経、康頼／必ず帰洛あるべしや、

赦免使、成経、康頼：必ず帰洛が叶うでしょう。	Amnesty officer, Naritsune, Yasuyori： Surely return home.

シテ／これは真か。

俊寛：これは真か？	Shunkan：Is that actually so?

赦免使、成経、康頼／なかなかに、

赦免使、成経、康頼：もちろんのこと	Amnesty officer, Naritsune, Yasuyori： Surely yes.

シテ／頼むぞよ頼もしくて、

俊寛：頼むぞ。頼もしく思っているぞ。	Shunkan：I really rely on you.

地／待てよ待てよと言ふ声も、姿も次第に、遠ざかる沖つ波の、幽かなる声絶えて、船影も人影も、消えて見えずになりにけり、跡消えて見えずになりにけり。

地謡：心強く待てよ、心強く待てよ。呼びかける声も一行の姿も次第に遠く幽かになり、静かな波音以外何も聞こえなくなった。船影も人影も何も見えなくなった。（終曲）	Chorus：Please wait patiently. Please wait patiently. Not only the calling but also their shapes are becoming remote to be fading. There are no sound but calm murmurings of the sea waves. The shape of the boat and persons have all disappeared.（The end）

P. 110　後の世を待たで鬼界が島守と

I have become an inhabitant of this hellish island.

小鍛冶
Kokaji

能：五番目物
Category：The fifth

P. 152　ちやうと打つ
The hammer-striking sounds

目　次

Contents

あらすじ

小鍛冶とは、製鐵を営む大鍛冶に対し、刀匠など鉄加工に従事する職人の謂いである。

平安朝中期、夢の告げを得た一条帝の勅命により、橘道成は高名な刀匠である三条の小鍛冶宗近邸に赴き、帝のための剣を打たせる。

宗近は相応しい相槌役がいないことに躊躇しつつも、遂に勅命に応ずる決意をする。

宗近は神力に縋ろうと、氏神の稲荷明神に参詣する。道すがら不思議な童子（前シテ）に遭遇するが、童子は宗近が剣製作の勅命を受けたことを既に知っていた。童子は漢家本朝の剣の威徳を物語り、宗近を励ます。童子はまた、相槌役を勤めることを約束し、鍛冶の壇をしつらえて待つよう伝えた後、稲荷山の山中に姿を消す。

宗近の従者（間狂言）の独白があり、それが終わると鍛冶装束に身を固めた宗近（後ワキ）が登場し、鍛冶の壇に上り神助の祈りを捧げる。

稲荷明神（後シテ）が現れ、宗近の相槌役を勤め、打ちあがった剣の裏に小狐丸と刻印し、それを勅使に捧げるや、稲荷山の山中に飛び入り姿を消す。

中啓童扇
Dou fan（used here by Douji）for Noh play

Outline

A Ko Kaji, or minor blacksmith, is a craftsman who forges swords and other relatively small iron goods, in contrast to Oh Kaji, or major blacksmith, which refers to iron industries.

In the mid-Heian period, the emperor Ichijou had a revelation in a dream. Upon Emperor's orders, Tachibana no Michinari (Waki tsure) went to visit the famous craftsman, Kokaji Munechika in Sanjo (Waki), in order to let him forge a sword for the Emperor.

Although Munechika hesitated to do that, because of a lack of an eligible partner, he at last decided to accept the order.

Munechika went to worship the local deity at the Inari shrine, to get god's help for his work. On the way to the shrine, he met a mysterious kid (Shi-te in the first half), who had known of the information that Munechika got the order from the Emperor to forge the sword.

The kid told Munechika stories about sword's virtues and influences in China and Japan, and encouraged him. The kid then promised to engage in the role of forging partner, suggested that Munechika prepare the platform, and disappeared into the Inari mountain. After the monologue by Munechika's attendant (Ai), Munechika (Waki in the second half), fully dressed in the forging outfits, reappears, mounts on the forging platform, and prays for god's help. Then the body of the Inari god (Shi-te in the second half) appears, and urges Munechika to forge the sword.

The god (Shi-te in the second half) engages the forging partner to Munechika, engraves the name of Ko Kitsune (small fox) on the back of the forged sword, gives it to the imperial messenger (Waki tsure), and disappears, flying into the Inari mountain.

注 記	
作 者	不詳
資 材	不明であるが、鎌倉時代後期に書かれた刀剣関連の古文書に三条の小鍛冶宗近の名が見える。
場 面	前場：伏見稲荷参道にある宗近の私邸。
	後場：前場と同じ。

登場人物		
名 前	役 柄	能 面
童子	前シテ	童子
稲荷明神	後シテ	小飛出
三条の小鍛冶 宗近	ワキ	無し
勅使	ワキツレ	無し
宗近の従者	間狂言	無し

童子面

Dōji mask

Notes	
Creator	Unknown
Materials	Unclear, but we can see the name of a craftsman, Kokaji Munechika in Sanjo, on a sword-relating ancient document written in the late Kamakura period.
Scenes	The first half : Munechika's residence, which is located on the way to Fushimi-Inari shrine
	The second half : The same as the first half

Characters		
Names	Role	Mask
A kid	Shi-te in the first half	Douji
The Inari god	Shi-te in the second half	Kotobide
The craftsman Kokaji Munechika in Sanjo	Waki	no mask
The imperial messenger	Wakitsure	no mask
Munechika's attendant	Ai	no mask

小飛出面
Kotobide mask

シーン1：勅使道成（ワキツレ）の登場

勅使橘の道成が幕から姿を現し、何事もなく橋掛りを進み、舞台に入り常座に立つ。軈て自らを名のり、勅命の趣を述べる。

Scene1：The Imperial messenger Michinari (Waki tsure) appears.

The Imperial messenger Tachibana no Michinari appears from behind the curtain, proceeds down the corridor, without any Hayashi music, enters the stage, and stands at the Johza. He then introduces himself and recites the purport of the Imperial order.

[名宣]
ワキツレ／これは一条の院に仕へ奉る橘の道成にて候、さても今夜帝不思議の御告ましますにより、三条の小鍛冶宗近を召し、御剣を打たせらるべきとの勅諚にて候間、只今宗近が私宅へと急ぎ候。

[名宣]

道成：これは一条帝にお仕えする橘道成であります。さて今夜帝は夢中に不思議なお告げを受けられた。帝には三条の小鍛冶宗近に命じ、帝の御為に剣を打たせるべしとの御諚であります。これより急ぎ宗近の私宅へ参ります。

[Self introduction]

Michinari：I'm Tachibana no Michinari, serving for the Emperor Ichijou. Well, His Majesty has had a mysterious revelation in his dream tonight. He wants to order the craftsman Kokaji Munechika in Sanjō to forge a sword for him. I'm in hurry to go to visit Munechika in his residence.

道成は橋掛り右手、一の松にて宗近に呼びかける。宗近は幕から姿を現し、橋掛り左手、三の松に立つ。両者は言葉を交わす。

二人の会話が済むと地謡が上歌の謡を謡う。謡の終わりに道成は舞台右手前のワキ座に座り、宗近は舞台左奥の常座に立つ。

Scene 2 : Dialogue between Michinari and Munechika (Waki).

Michinari calls out to Munechika at the Ichi no Matsu, at the right of the corridor. Munechika appears from behind the curtain and stands at the San no Matsu, at the left of the corridor. They have a conversation. After the conversation, the chorus sings uptone. At the end of the song, Michinari sits at the Wakiza, front stage right, and Munechika stands at the Johza, back stage left.

ワキツレ／いかにこの家の内に宗近があるか。

道成：やあやあ宗近殿はご在宅か？	Michinari：Hello there. Is Munechika in?

ワキ／宗近とは誰にて渡り候ぞ。

宗近：宗近と呼ばれるのは何方様でしょうか？	Munechika：Who is calling me, as Munechika?

ワキツレ／これは一条の院の勅使にてあるぞとよ、さても帝今夜不思議の御告ましますに依り、宗近を召し御剣を打たせらるべきとの勅諚なり、急いで仕り候へ。

道成：これは一条帝の勅使である。さて帝におかれては今夜夢中に不思議なお告げを受けられ、汝、宗近に命じて帝	Michinari：I'm an Imperial messenger from the Emperor Ichijou. Well, His Majesty has had a mysterious revelation in his dream tonight, and he wants to order you, Munechika,

のために剣を打たせるべしと
の勅諚である。急いでご奉仕
申し上げよ。

to forge a sword for him. Get ready to do it in
a hurry.

ワキ〳宣旨畏つて承り候、さやうの御剣を仕るべきには、我に劣らぬ者相槌
を仕りてこそ、御剣も成就候べけれ、これはとかくの御返事を、申しかねた
るばかりなり。

宗近：宣旨は確かに承りまし
た。しかしながら、そのような
特別な剣をお打ち申すには、我
に劣らぬ相応の技量を持つ相
槌役が必要です。お受けでき
るか確とご返事致しかねます。

Munechika：I've heard His Majesty's orders.
However, I know that I need an eligible
partner with no less skill than I have, to forge
such a special sword. So, I'm not sure I can
accept the order.

ワキツレ〳げにげに汝が申す所は理なれども、帝不思議の御告ましませば、頼
もしく思ひつつ、はやはや領状申すべしと、重ねて宣旨ありければ。

道成：其方の申されることは
もっともであるが、帝は不思
議の御告げを受けてお命じな
されていることである。しか
らば尚々急ぎお受けされよ。

Michinari：Though, I understand what
you're saying, the order is based on His
Majesty's mysterious revelation. So, again, I
urge you to accept right away.

［上歌］
ワキ〳この上は、ともかくにも宗近が、

［上歌の謡］
宗近：この上はお受けするほ
かあるまい、と。

[Sing uptone]
Munechika：In this situation, I have no
choice but to comply.

138

地/とにもかくにも宗近が、進退ここにきはまりて、御剣の刃の、乱るる心なりけり。さりながら御政道、直なる今の御代なれば、若しも奇特のありやせん、それのみ頼む心かな、それのみ頼む心かな。

地謡：宗近は進退窮まって、なすすべもなく刃の乱れ焼きになるが如く困惑するのだった。しかしながら、今は御政道の正しい御代なので、神仏のご加護による奇跡もあるかも知れない。宗近はそれのみを頼りに、それのみを頼りにするのだった。

Chorus：He, Munechika, can't help being at an impasse, is at a loss how to act, bewildered as though there were forging failure. However, It's been the right Emperor reigning now, so he may expect miraculous assistance from the gods. Munechika just relies on that. Munechika just relies on that.

シーン3：宗近の独白

宗近は常座に立ち、困惑した体で独り言ちる。やがて日頃から帰依する伏見稲荷神社に参拝することを決意する。独白の終わりにシテの出の幕が上がる。

Scene 3 : Munechika's monologue.

Munechika (Waki) talks to himself, standing at the Johza. He seems bewildered, and then he determines to visit Fushimi-Inari shrine, to which he has had religious devotion his whole life. At the end of his monologue, the curtain rises, and we can anticipate Shi-te's appearance.

ワキ/言語道断、一大事を仰せ出されて候ものかな、かやうの御事は神力をたのみ申すならではと存じ候、某が氏の神は稲荷の明神なれば、これより直に稲荷に参り、祈誓申さばやと存じ候。

宗近：なんともはや大変な難題をお命じになったものだ。これは神助を頼むほかはある

Munechika：What extremely Majesty ordered! I can't help but rely on the gods' help to do this. My tutelary deity is the Inari

まい。我が氏神は稲荷明神な | god. So, I'd like to visit Inari shrine right
ので、すぐに稲荷神社にお助 | away to ask for help.
けを頼みに参詣しようと思う。

シーン4：シテの登場

童子の面をつけ、黒頭を被った化人風のシテが幕の中から声をかけ宗近を呼び止める。宗近は童子の異形の風体と、すべてを知るかのような言葉を訝しむ。

やがて童子は橋掛りを進み、舞台に入る。両人の対話が終わると、地謡が上歌の謡を謡う。上歌の間、童子は舞台上を回り、奇跡が起こるであろうことを示唆する。

Scene 4 : Shi-te appears.

A phantom-like kid (Shi-te) with a Douji mask and long black hair (Kuro-Gashira), calls from behind the curtain to halt Munechika. Munechika feels wonder at seeing the kid's extraordinary figure and to hear it speaks in a way that implies it knows everything. The kid then proceeds down the corridor, and enters the stage. After the dialogue between the two of them, the chorus starts to sing uptone. Through the uptone song, the kid steps around the stage, suggesting that a miracle is happening.

シテ／なうなうあれなるは三条の小鍛冶宗近にて御入り候か。

童子：やあやあ、其方は三条 | The kid：Hello there. Are you Kokaji
の小鍛冶宗近殿ではないか？ | Munechika from Sanjō?

ワキ／不思議やななべてならざる御事の、我が名をさして宣ふは、如何なる人にてましますぞ。

宗近：不思議なことだ。異形 | Munechika：It's a wonder. Who on earth are
の風体で私のことを呼ばれる | you, this extraordinary-looking person who
貴方様は、一体何方でしょう？ | calls to me?

140

シテ／雲の上なる帝より、剣を打ちて参らせよと、汝に仰せありしよなう、

童子：帝より剣を打てとの勅 命があったよな？

The kid：The Emperor ordered you to forge a sword for him, didn't he?

ワキ／さればこそそれにつけてもなほなほ不思議の御事かな、剣の勅も只今なるを、早くも知ろし召さるる事、返すがへすも不審なり、

宗近：おお、そのことまでご 存知とは。やはり不思議なお 方だ。勅命があったのはつい 先程のことなのに、既にそのこ とをご存知とは訝しいことだ。

Munechika：Oh, you know about that. What a wonder you are! It's nothing but dubious that you already know about the Imperial order, despite it happening a few minutes ago.

シテ／げにげに不審はさる事なれども、我のみ知れば外人までも、

童子：其方が不審に思うのは もっともだが、我一人知ると いうことは諸人までも……

The kid：Your suspicion is natural. However, my knowing may mean that the other people may, too.

ワキ／天に声あり、

宗近：天に声あれば……

Munechika：If there is a heavenly voice,

シテ／地に響く、

童子：至る所に伝わるようで ……

The kid：It may prevail all over the world.

地〳壁に耳、岩の物言ふ世の中に、岩の物言ふ世の中に、隠れはあらじ殊にな
ほ、雲の上人の御剣の、光は何か暗からん。ただ頼めこの君の、恵みによらば
御剣も、などか心に叶はざる、などかは叶はざるべき。

[上歌の謡]

地謡：壁に耳あり、岩がもの
言うという。この世では秘め
事もたやすく、あまねく知れ
渡るものだ。殊に剣の一件は
勅命に関わることであり、隠
し通すにはあまりに顕著な事
柄である。ただ帝のご威光を
頼みにされよ。必ず、心に叶
う出来栄えとなろう。心に叶
う出来栄えとなろう。

[Sing uptone]

Chorus：They say either that walls have
ears, or that rocks have mouths. In this world,
secrets easily tend to prevail everywhere.
The sword matter, especially, concerning His
Majesty's order, is too conspicuous to conceal.
You should just rely on His Majesty's
authority. You must do it in a satisfactory
way. You must do it in a satisfactory way.

シーン5：童子の物語

宗近は地謡前、童子は舞台中央に座っている。童子と地謡がこれより交互にクリ、サシ、クセの謡を
謡い、その中で漢家、本朝での剣の霊験や日本武尊の物語などを述べる。
クセの謡の中で童子は「尊は剣を抜いて」と謡って立ち、物語をなぞる所作を演ずる。物語の終わり
に童子は宗近に語りかけつつ再び座る。

Scene 5 : The kid (Shi-te) tells the story.

Munechika now sits in front of the chorus troupe. The kid sits at stage
center. The kid and the chorus, then, in turn sing Kuri, Sashi and Kuse songs,
including the story about the miracles, which happened concerning China's
and Japan's swords, and also the story about the lord, " Yamato Takeru".
During the Kuse song, the kid stands up at the point, "the lord draws his
sword", and then starts to perform actions, simulating the story. At the end
of the story, he sits again, calling to Munechika.

［クリ］

地／それ漢王三尺の剣、居ながら秦の乱れを治め、また煬帝がけいの剣、周室の光を奪へり。

［クリの謡］

地謡：そもそも漢の高祖が秦末の乱世を鎮めたのは三尺の剣の威徳であった。また、隋朝の煬帝の「けいの剣」は北周の命脈を絶った。

[Kuri song]

Chorus：Well then, the First Emperor of the Former Han Dynasty rectified the turbulence at the end of Qin Dynasty, thanks to Sanseki sword's virtue and influence. Then, the Kei sword, which belonged to Emperor Yang of the Sui dynasty, took the Northern Zhou's life.

［サシ］

シテ／その後玄宗皇帝の鐘馗大臣も、

［サシの謡］

童子：その後唐の玄宗皇帝の鐘馗大臣も……

[Sashi Song]

The kid：After that, the minister Zhong Kui in Emperor Hsuan Tsung's period (Tang Dynasty) also,

地／剣の徳に魂魄は、君辺に仕え奉り、

地謡：その死後までも剣の力を以て魂魄が帝をお守りし……

Chorus：guarded His Majesty with his sword's power, even after his own death.

シテ／魍魎鬼神に至るまで、

童子：そのために悪霊や鬼神の類まで、

The kid：So, even evil spirits,

地／剣の刃の光に恐れて、その仇をなす事を得ず、

地謡：剣の霊力を恐れて災いを及ぼすことができなかった。	Chorus：devils and that sort of thing couldn't inflict destruction on him, fearful of the miracle sword's influences.

シテ／漢家本朝に於いて剣の威徳、

童子：漢家本朝において剣の威徳というものは…	The kid：Both in China and in our country, sword' miracle influences,

地／申すに及ばぬ奇特とかや。

地謡：言うまでもなく有難く貴重なのである。	Chorus：as we all know, are beneficial and precious.

［クセ］

地／また我が朝のその始め、人皇十二代、景行天皇、皇子の尊の御名をば、日本武と申ししが、東夷を退治の勅を受け、関の東も遥かなる、東の旅の道すがら、伊勢や尾張の、海面に立つ波までも、帰る事よと羨み、何時か我も帰る波の、衣手にあらめやと、思ひつづけて行く程に。

［クセの謡］

地謡：そもそも我が朝の始祖神武帝より十二代下った景行天皇の皇子で日本武と申される御方が、帝より東夷を平らげるべしとの命を受け、逢坂の関を遥かに越えて東征された。進むうち伊勢や尾張の岸辺に打ち返す波を見て、自分も帰還できればと羨みながらも、いつかは凱旋を果たすべしと心に誓いつつ進むうちに……	[Kuse song] Chorus：Well then, the son of Emperor Keiko, who was a descendant of the twelfth generation of the first Emperor Jinmu, called the lord Yamato Takeru, advanced his army toward the far eastern province beyond the Ohsaka Barrier, on orders from the Emperor to destroy the eastern barbarians. While advancing on, he had the feeling of longing to return, much like the waves receding from the shores in Ise and Owari. However, he forced himself to proceed, while vowing to

144

make a triumphant return some day.

シテ／其処や此処の戦ひに、

童子：其処此処で戦いがあり……

地／人馬岩窟に身を砕き、血は涿鹿の川となつて、紅波楯流し、数度に及べる夷も、兜を脱いで矛を伏せ、みな降参を申しけり、またこの御宇より、御狩場を始め給へり。頃は神無月。二十日あまりの事なれば。四方の紅葉も冬枯の遠山にかかる薄雪を。眺めさせ給ひしに。

地謡：人馬は敵の岩窟に苦闘し、血は川のようになって流れた。それは宛ら古代中国の黄帝と蚩尤の涿鹿の戦いの如くであった。
ために味方の盾も紅に波打つこと数度に及んだが、遂には敵は兜を脱ぎ、武器を捨てたのだった。因みに御狩場というのはこの御代に始まっている。
時は十月二十日余りのこと、御狩場の四方も冬枯れて尊は遠山にかかる薄雪を眺めておられた。

Chorus：The horses and riders struggled to fight in the enemy's rocky fortress, and the blood that was shed formed what looked like a stream. It was like the ancient battle between Emperor Huang-di and Chi-Yuri in the Takuroku battlefield in China. As a result, his army's shields became bent like crimson waves several times, but at last the enemy was subdued, and eventually disarmed. By the way, a hunting- fields have their origin in this reign. The time was around October 20th or after, and the scene was wintry and desolate in the hunting-field. Then he was taking a look at the distant mountains with light, snow-capped peaks, when

シテ／夷四方を囲みつつ、

童子：夷どもが四方を囲み……

The kid：the barbarians besieged us,

地／枯野の草に火をかけ、余焰頻りに燃え上り、敵攻鼓を打ちかけて、火焔を放ちて懸りければ。

地謡：枯野の草に火をかけ、為に炎が燃え上がった。敵は攻め鼓を打ち鳴らし、火焔によって我らに襲いかかった。

Chorus：and set fire to the dried-up grass in the field, so that it burst into flame. The enemy beat the attack drum, and tried to destroy us by fire.

シテ／尊は剣を抜いて、

童子：尊は剣を抜いて……

The kid：Then, the lord drew his sword.

地／尊は剣を抜いて、辺を払ひ忽ちに、焔も立ち退けと、四方の草を薙ぎ払へば、剣の精霊嵐となって、焔も草も吹き返されて、天に輝き地に充ち満ちて、猛火は却つて敵を焼けば、数万騎の夷どもは、忽ち此処にて失せてげり。その後四海治まりて、人家戸ざしを忘れしも、その草薙の故とかや、只今、汝が打つべき、その瑞相の御剣も、いかでそれには劣るべき、伝ふる家の宗近よ、心やすくも、思ひて下向し給へ。

地謡：尊は剣を抜いて、辺りを切り払った。すぐに炎を払いのけようと辺りの草を刈り除けるのだった。剣の精霊は嵐を起こし、刈り除けた草もろともに炎を吹き返した。為に枯野は猛火に包まれて数万に及ぶ夷どもはたちまち此処にて滅び去った。この後あまねく平和が訪れ、人々は戸締まりを忘れ、平穏を楽しんだのである。これも草薙の剣の威徳であると伝え

Chorus：The lord drew his sword to cut and clear surroundings. He mowed down the surrounding grass, in order to expel the fire immediately. The mysterious spirit of the sword then, evoked a storm and drove back fire, along with the mowed grass. As a result, the field were engulfed in the fierce flame that burned out adversaries, and immediately destroyed the barbarians who numbered in the tens of thousands. After that, peace reigned all over the country, and people enjoyed the blessings of peace, without suffering from robberies. They said it was thanks to the

られる。汝が勅命を受けて打つ剣も、その力は草薙の剣に劣ることはあるまい。汝宗近は刀匠の家の奥義を受け継ぐ者、安んじて家路に就かれよ。

power of the sword Kusanagi (mowing grass). The power of the sword, which you were ordered by His Majesty to forge, should be as strong as the sword Kusanagi. You, Munechika, who has inherited the craftsman's arcane, better get home, and take it easy.

シーン6：童子の中入り

童子（シテ）は宗近（ワキ）に対面して座り、問答となる。
宗近が喜ぶのを聞いて、童子は上歌の謡で立ち、常座に行く。軈て童子は宗近に剣を打つ準備をするよう促し、幕に走り込む。(中入り)
稲荷山に姿を隠す風情である。
宗近は立ってそれを見送り、続いて中入りする。

Scene 6 : The kid takes leave of the stage.
The kid (Shi-te) sits facing Munechika (Waki), and the two of them start conversing. After hearing Munechika's delightful words, the kid stands up to move toward the Johza, accompanied by an uptone song. The kid then urges Munechika to make preparations for forging the sword, and runs inside the curtain (taking leave). It looks like he is off to hide in the Inari mountain. Munechika stands up to follow the kid with his eyes, and follows the kid into intermission.

ワキ／漢家本朝に於いて剣の威徳、時にとつての祝言なり、さてさて御身は如何なる人ぞ、

宗近：漢家本朝の剣の威徳の物語をお聞きして、今この時に有難いことでした。貴方は一体何方様でしょうか？

Munechika：I'm really delighted to hear from you the stories about the miracle sword's power both
in Caina and in our country, from you at the convenient time for me. Who on earth are you?

シテ／よし誰とてもただ頼め、まづまづ勅の御剣を、打つべき壇を飾りつつ、その時我を待ち給はば、

童子：我が誰であってもただ我を頼め。まずは勅命の御剣を打つ鍛冶壇を壮麗に整えて我をお待ちあれ。

The kid：No matter who I am, you had better rely on me. First of all, you should prepare the platform in splendid fashion for forging the sword and wait for my appearance.

［上歌］
地／通力の身を変じ、通力の身を変じて、必ずその時節に、参り会ひて御力を、つけ申すべし待ち給へと、夕雲の稲荷山、行方も知らず失せにけり、行方も知らず失せにけり。

［上歌の謡］
地謡：我は神通力を顕し、神通力を顕して、必ず汝の助勢に参り会いましょう。我の参会をお待ちあれというや、稲荷山の方へ行くと見えて、行き方知れず消え失せた、行き方知れず消え失せた。

[Sing uptone]
Chorus：I'll then reveal my supernatural substance, I'll then reveal my supernatural substance, and surely make an appearance to assist you. No sooner does the kid say that you should wait for his appearance, than he looks like he is leaving toward the Inari mountain, where he disappears to nowhere, disappears to nowhere.

シーン7：間狂言のシャベリ

(能の前場と後場の幕間に狂言方が前場の出来事を略述する) 稲荷山の麓に住む里人が出て、宗近の従者であると名のり、前場の出来事とほぼ同様の物語を語って、退場する。(狂言のシャベリの内容自体は掲載されない)

Scene 7 : Ai-kyōgen's talk.

(an explanatory interlude between the two halves of a Noh play performed by Kyōgen-kata, comedic performers in Noh. A villager who lives at the foot of Inari mountain (Ai), introduces himself as Munechika's attendant, tells the story which is almost the same as the story in the first half, and exits the stage. (Kyōgen's monologue itself isn't written in the text)

シーン8：後ワキの登場

後見が舞台の中央前に一畳台を置く。台には、前方に注連縄（聖域を結界するためのロープ）を張り巡らし、金床、刀身、槌、御幣が置かれている。宗近（後ワキ）がノットの囃子に導かれて幕から姿を現す。烏帽子をつけた正装である。橋掛りを進み、舞台に入り、壇に上がる。やがて「謹上再拝」と唱え、壇上に座る。

Scene 8 : Waki in the second half appears.

Kohken (stage attendant) sets Ichi-joh-Dai (a platform) at front-center stage. On the platform, Shimenawa (a rope used to cordon off consecrated areas) is stretched around at the front side, and several tools are placed there, an anvil, a sword blade, a hammer, and Gohei (sacred paper strips). Munechika (Waki in the second half) appears from behind the curtain, accompanied by Notto music by Hayashi. Dressed in formal attire with Kazaori Eboshi (a formal cap), he proceeds down the corridor, enters the stage, and mounts on the platform. He then sings "Kinjou Saihai" (praying sincerely), and sits on the platform.

ワキ／宗近勅に従つて、即ち壇に上りつつ、不浄を隔つる七重の注連、四方に本尊を懸け奉り、幣帛を捧げ、仰ぎ願はくは、宗近時に至つて、人皇六十六代一条の院の御宇に、その職の誉を蒙る事、これ私の力にあらず、伊弉諾伊弉冉の天の浮橋を踏み渡り、豊芦原を探り給ひし御矛より始まれり、その後南瞻僧伽陀国、波斯弥陀尊者よりこの方、天国ひつきの子孫に伝へて今に至れり、

宗近：我宗近はただちに壇に上がり、不浄を隔てる七重の注連縄を回らしてその四方に稲荷明神像を掲げ……謹んで願い奉る。

我宗近は今この時、人皇六十六代一条帝の御代に刀工としての栄誉を蒙りました。

そもそも刀鍛冶の起こりは天の御矛に始まり、それによって伊弉諾、伊弉冉の二神が天の浮橋を渡られ、豊芦原中つ国をお造りになった。

その後南瞻部洲の僧伽陀国の波斯弥陀尊者を経由して、古代からの刀工の祖、天国や日継の技をその子孫たちに伝えたのである。願わくは……

Munechika：Myself Munechika, will immediately mount the platform, stretch around the ropes (Shimenawa) seven-fold in order to cordon off evil, put up the Inari god's figures at each corners of the ropes, and hold up a Gohei. I sincerely ask for your kind help. Myself, Munechika, has received honours as a craftsman in the regin of the present 66th emperor, Ichijou. This is not the result of my own effort. Well then, the sword- forging has its origin in the Holy Pike (Amano Mihoko), with which the two Gods, Izanagi and Izanami, crossed over the Heaven's Bridge (Amano Ukihashi) to create our Toyo Ashiwara country. After that, they passed down to their descendants the craftsmanship of the ancestors from ancient times, Amakuni and Hitsuki, via saint Hashimida in Sou-Kata country, in Nansen Province. I ask for,

地／願はくは、宗近私の、功名にあらず、普天率士の、勅命に依れり、さあらば十方、恒沙の諸神、只今の宗近に、力を合はせて、賜び給へとて、幣帛を捧げつつ、天に仰ぎ、頭を地につけ、骨髄の丹誠、聞き入れ納受、せしめ給へや。

地謡：願わくは、全宇宙の神々よ、我を助けたまえ。こ

Chorus：I ask for your kind help, myriads gods of the cosmos. This isn't for my own

のことは宗近自身の功名のた
めではなく、全国土を統べら
れる帝のご命令によるもので
す。なので全宇宙の神々には
この宗近に今お力をお貸しく
ださい。と我は御幣を掲げ、
天を仰ぎ、頭を地につけて祈
る。どうか我が心底からの懇
願をお聞き入れください。

personal exploits, but as ordered by His
Majesty, who reigns over our whole country.
So, give me, Munechika, your special aid right
now. I'm holding a Gohei up, praying with my
face up toward the heavens and my head
down toward the ground. Please listen to my
sincere imploring.

ワキ／謹上再拝。（キンジョオサイハイ）

宗近：謹上再拝。

Munechika：I'm sincerely praying for your
aid.（Kinjou Saihai）

シーン9：稲荷明神の登場

稲荷明神（後シテ）が早笛の演奏に導かれて幕から姿を現す。赤頭に狐戴輪冠を頂き、小飛出の面を
つけ、異界からの到来を思わせる装束（上半身は法被、下半身は半切）を纏い、手には槌を持つ。勢
いよく橋掛りを進み、舞台に入り常座に立つ。やがてリズム良く足拍子を踏み鳴らしながら宗近に呼
びかけ、力強い舞働の囃子に合わせて所作をする。

Scene 9 : The Inari god appears.

*The Inari god (Shi-te in the second half) appears from behind the curtain,
accompanied by Hayafue music, played by Hayashi. He wears red hair
(Akagashira) with a fox-figured pattern on the top of his head, the Ko Tobide
mask on his face, with a costume that looks like some kind of creature from
the spiritual world (the Happi for his upper garment and the Hangire for his
lower garment), and he holds a hammer in his hand. He vigorously proceeds
down the corridor, enters the stage, and stands at the Johza. He then calls
out to Munechika while stomping rhythmically, and performs a dance
accompanied by Mai Hataraki music, powerfully played by Hayashi.*

地／いかにや宗近、勅《チョク》の剣《ツルギ》、いかにや宗近、勅の剣、打つべき時節は、虚空に知れり、頼《タノ》めや頼め、ただ頼め。

地謡：如何に宗近、如何に宗近。剣を打つべき時が来た、時が来た。勅命の剣の鍛冶を始めよ。ただ我を頼め、我を頼め。（舞働の所作）	Chorus：Hail Munechika, Hail Munechika, I've known that, I've known that the time has just now come. You should start forging the sword that was ordered by his Majesty ; you can believe in my aid. Just believe me. (Mai Hataraki dance)

後シテ／童男壇《トオナンダン》の、上に上《ウエアガ》り、

稲荷明神：少年姿の稲荷明神は壇に上がり……	The Inari god：A boyish figure of the deity mounts on the platform.

地／童男壇の、上に上つて、宗近に三拝《サンパイ》の、膝《ヒザ》を屈《クツ》し、さて御剣の、鉄《カネ》はと問《ト》へば、宗近も恐悦《キョオエツ》の、心を先《サキ》として、鉄取り出し、教《ヲシエ》への槌《ツチ》を、はつたと打てば、

地謡：少年姿の稲荷明神は壇に上がって、刀鍛冶の師宗近に膝を屈して三拝し、さて打つべき鉄は？　と問う。宗近は大いに喜び鉄を取り出し、相槌を導く教えの初槌をはたと打てば……	Chorus：The boyish figure of the deity mounts on the platform, bows on his knee three times to Munechika, who is the master of sword- forging. It then asks Munechika which the iron for forging is. Munechika brings out the iron with great joy, and makes the first forging- strike, which will lead the partner's second strike.

シテ／ちやうと打つ《チョオ》、

稲荷明神：相槌をちょうと打ち……	The Inari god：Myself, the partner then makes the second strike, clang!

地：ちやうちやうちやうと、打ち重ねたる、槌の音、天地に響きて、おびたたしや。

地謡：ちょう！ ちょう！ と槌の音が勢いよく天地に響き渡った。

Chorus：The hammer-striking sounds vigorously, echoing all around the world. Clang, clang!

シーン10：結末

宗近と稲荷明神はそれぞれの名前を刀身に刻印する。宗近は剣を稲荷明神に手渡し、ともに壇を降りる。剣の完成を嘉するいくつかの所作の後稲荷明神はワキ座に座っている道成（ワキツレ）に剣を捧げる。軈て稲荷明神は橋掛りを下がり、幕近くで留拍子を踏む。

Scene10：Ending

Munechika and the Inari god each engrave their names on the sword. Munechika hands the Inari god the sword, dismounts from the platform together with him. After several actions which show appreciation to their accomplishment, the Inari god gives it to Michinari (Wakitsure), who sits at the Wakiza. The Inari god then proceeds down the corridor, and makes a ending stamp (Tome hyoushi) near the curtain.

ワキ／かくて御剣を打ち奉り、表に小鍛冶宗近と打つ、

宗近：かくて御剣を打ち奉り、我が名をその面に打つ。

Munechika：Thus, I have finished forging the sword and I have engraved my name on its surface.

シテ／神体時の弟子なれば、子狐と裏に鮮かに、

稲荷明神：我、稲荷明神は宗近殿の一時の弟子なので、裏に「小狐」と我が本名を打つ。

The Inari god：I, the god himself, clearly engraved my real name, "small fox", on the back surface, as Munechika's temporary partner.

地／打ち奉る御剣の、刃は雲を乱したれば、天の叢雲ともこれなれや。

地謡：御剣を打ち奉り、その表には雲形が出ているので、丸で名高い天の叢雲の剣とそっくりである。

Chorus：The sword has been forged, to have a cloud-figure pattern on its surface, so it looks similar to the famous sword, Ama no murakumo (meaning "clouds in heaven").

シテ／天下第一の、

稲荷明神：これは天下第一の……

The Inari god：This is paramount among all the swords.

地：天下第一の、二つ銘の御剣にて、四海を治め給へば、五穀成就もこの時なれや、即ち汝が氏の神、稲荷の神体小狐丸を、勅使に捧げ申し、これまでなりと言い捨てて、また叢雲に飛び乗り、また叢雲に、飛び乗りて東山、稲荷の峯にぞ帰りける。

地謡：これは天下第一の二つ銘の御剣で、四海に囲まれたこの国に平和を齎し、五穀成就を享受させる。我は汝宗近を守護する氏神である、と言い、やがて名剣小狐丸を勅使に捧げさらばと言い、また叢雲に、また叢雲に飛び乗って、稲荷山に帰って行った。（終曲）

Chorus：This is paramount among all the swords, the number one sword, with two names engraved on it, and it is able to keep peace all over the country that is surrounded by the sea of the four directions. The country then may enjoy a huge harvest of the five grains, in peace. The god is saying that he is no-one but the local deity who is protecting Munechika. He then gives the Imperial messenger the sword, excellent small fox sword (Ko kitsune maru), says good bye, and goes back to the Inari mountain, while riding again upon a surging cloud, while riding again upon a surging cloud. (The end)

前シテ

Shi-te in the first half

List of English Noh Script

能楽の英訳書籍一覧

Items 項目	by Waley ウェーレー訳		by Committee of Japan Society 日本学術振興会訳	by yosuke Nakano 中野訳
Title	The Noh Play of Japan		The Noh Drama Ten Plays from the Japanese	Noh 5 Scripts in English ―対訳能五番―
Year of Published 発行年 Publisher 発行者	First edition, 1921 by Unwin, London First Tuttle Edition, 1976		Tuttle, 1955	this book 本書
ISBN	978-4-8053-1033-5		804804281	978-4-286-21323-1
Number of Plays 収録曲数	19		10	5（Published）/10（Translated）
Name of contained Pieces 収録曲名	Atsumori 敦盛	Ikuta 生田	Takasago 高砂	Takasago The first 高砂（初番目物）
	Tsunemasa 経正	Kumasaka 熊坂	Tamura 田村	Kiyotsune The second 清経（二番目物）
	Eboshiori 烏帽子折	Hashibenkei 橋弁慶	Sanemori 実盛	Hajitomi The Third 半蔀（三番目物）
	Kagekiyo 景清	Hachinoki 鉢木	Kiyotsune 清経	Shunkan The 4th 俊寛（四番目物）
	Sotowakomachi 卒塔婆小町	Ukai 鵜飼	Touboku 東北	Kokaji The 5th 小鍛冶（切能）
	Ayanotsuzumi 綾鼓	Aoinoue 葵上	Izutsu 井筒	Izutsu 井筒
	Kantan 邯鄲	Houkazou 放下僧	Eguchi 江口	Hagoromo 羽衣
	Hagoromo 羽衣	Tanikou 谷行	Bashou 芭蕉	**Kagetsu 花月**
	Ikenie 生贄	Hatsuyuki 初雪	Sumidagawa 隅田川	**Makiginu 巻絹**
	Hakurakuten 白楽天	Sammaries of 16 Pieces 要約16番	Funabenkei 船弁慶	**Kayoikomachi 通小町**

中野訳覧のアンダーラインを引いたものは今回収録した能5番、太字は中野既訳でこれまでに英訳がなされていない能本を示す。

In "by Yosuke Nakano" column, 5 pieces in the underlined letters are now published, and another 3 pieces in bold characters are the first translations of them in the world.

著者プロフィール

中野 洋介 （なかの ようすけ）

1936 年大阪府生。大阪大法学部卒。40 余年電力会社に在職　管理職の傍ら能楽観世流　故河村禎二師に師事。1992 年師範認定。趣味の英語学習で 2017 年英検準一級。
（ウエブサイト URL：http://yoginkai.site/　からその他の能の英訳スクリプトをご覧になれます）

Author's Biography

Nakano Yosuke

Nakano Yosuke was born in 1936 in Osaka Prefecture. He graduated from Osaka University's Faculty of Law, and worked at an electric power company for over 40 years. While working in a managerial position, he started studying under the renowned, late Teiji Kawamura at the Kanze Noh School. He became certified as a Kanze Noh instructor 1992. Regarding English as one of his extracurricular interests, he became certified in Eiken (Test in Practical English Proficiency), Grade Pre-1 in 2017.
(You can review another couple of Noh scripts in English from my webpageURL： http://yoginkai.site/)

Noh 5 Scripts in English　—対訳能五番—

2020年 9 月15日　初版第 1 刷発行

著　者　中野 洋介
発行者　瓜谷 綱延
発行所　株式会社文芸社
　　　　〒160-0022　東京都新宿区新宿1－10－1
　　　　　　　　　電話 03-5369-3060（代表）
　　　　　　　　　　　 03-5369-2299（販売）

印刷所　図書印刷株式会社

©Nakano Yosuke 2020 Printed in Japan
乱丁本・落丁本はお手数ですが小社販売部宛にお送りください。
送料小社負担にてお取り替えいたします。
本書の一部、あるいは全部を無断で複写・複製・転載・放映、データ配信することは、法律で認められた場合を除き、著作権の侵害となります。
ISBN978-4-286-21323-1